Corporate Banking

(A guide book for Novice)

*

by

Dr. Ramamurthy N

M.Sc., B.G.L., C.A.I.I.B., C.C.P., D.S.A.D.P., C.I.S.A., P.M.P., CGBL, Ph.D.

*

2013

Name of the Book: **Corporate Banking**
(A guide book for Novice)

First Edition: 2013

Author: **Dr. Ramamurthy N,**
http://ramamurthy.jaagruti.co.in/

ISBN(13): 978-93-82237-08-2

Number of Pages: 206

*****

TABLE OF CONTENTS

*****

Dedication

I dedicate this book to the Global Banking Industry which brought me to this level.

Dr. Ramamurthy N

*****

M.P. Sivan Arul M.B.A., B.L., C.A.I.I.B. Special Officer

Foreword

I am quite happy to write a foreword to this book on "Corporate Banking". As a cooperative banker, I have realized how essential it is for the banking personnel to keep themselves abreast of all the challenging changes happening in the Banking Industry in the wake of globalization. Mr. **N. Ramamurthy**, author of this book, erstwhile banker, a consultant and a research scholar, is a post-graduate in Mathematics and a Certified Associate of Indian Institute of Bankers. His work experience in various areas of banking and his quest for learning and fondness for teaching have helped him to develop mastery over the subject systematically with comparative financial systems, particularly with more focus on emerging markets. This book would not have been possible but for the strong grasp of banking practices that the author has.

Corporate sector is in the midst of rapid flux as it is growing rapidly, both in the scale and in the diversity of actors, and is sitting on the cusp of regulation. This book is an attempt to put together a one-stop reference that will help a variety of readers catch up on the issues of corporate financing, as it has a comprehensive coverage. The book offers conceptual clarity with emphasis on a student-friendly approach and is an attempt at demystifying the tough subject. The book includes a glossary of terms and some pictorial representations for a better understanding of the concepts discussed.

Its language is lucid and the difficult concepts of finance theory have been simplified with the help of illustrations and practical examples. It is a theory book with a practical bias, displaying the author's personal experience. Though the author has stated in his preface that the book aims at customers, I would recommend **"Corporate Banking"** as a **'must'** read for the bankers as well. The book is a snapshot of the wholesale banking activity to be of use to the readers to understand the concepts in the proper perspective. While parts of it have been overtaken by events, most of the items and analysis will remain relevant for time to come and I expect it to retain permanent value as a book for quick reference.

Chennai
04th May 2012

M.P. Sivan Arul
Special Officer
The Tamilnadu State Apex Co-operative Bank Ltd.

*****

Preface

Earlier the banking industry was service oriented – they had different counters for Savings, Term Deposit, Current Account, etc. But after the advent of Core Banking System, thanks to Western Banking, it all has become product oriented – Retail, Corporate, etc. The banks do not have clients for their services, but have customers, instead, for their products. The facet of the entire banking industry across the globe is undergoing a thorough manifestation.

At a higher plane, banks offer their customers portfolio management services. When banking transcends beyond a level, it metamorphoses into private banking. In simple terms it can be understood that Retail Banking deals with individual customers and Corporate Banking deals with business entities. Normally Banks do have a cluster of deposit products to Retail Customers and lending products to Corporate Customers. Hence Corporate Banking mostly deals with Credit.

Is Appraising of Credit to Corporates by banks an 'Art' or 'Science'? If it is a science automated systems can take care of it. If it is art there could no help from any type of systems. It is blend of both. It is an art – interview of the prospective borrower by the bankers is a must to assess the capability and intent of the loan applicants. However, it has to be supported by various projected financial statements, ratios, etc., which systems can only support with accurate calculations.

The author has experienced three different perspectives about banking as:

- Manual Banking process
- Using automated banking process
- Offering IT solutions to automate banking processes across the globe

Various trainees, who attended the author's various training programmes under banking, requested him to write a general book about **Corporate Banking**. This book is aimed at the audience of bankers and non-bankers.

While primarily this book deals with Corporate Banking areas viz., Working Capital, Trade Finance, Foreign Exchange, etc., the current trends in Banking like Financial Inclusion, Islamic Banking, Channel of Banking, Banking Landscape, AML, etc., are also discussed. Overview of Banking Treasury and Risk Management are also covered to give a perspective to the readers. Separate books on **Retail Banking, Corporate Finance and Banking GRC** have been written by the same author covers on other areas of Banking. Another book **Dictionary of Financial Terms** explains various global banking concepts, jargons and acronyms.

There is subtle difference in Banking Theory, Law and Practice. Those are also noted in this book wherever possible. Now, since the banking is more of product oriented, it needs marketing also. Hence a chapter on Bank Marketing is also added. Presently the banking is no more account related – it is all marketing, relationship and a kind of computer operation. Hence this chapter is more apt and relevant in the current trend.

This book mainly talks about Indian banking system, of course, the root of which is British system. However, with the world-wide experience of the author, almost all the areas are compared with global banking scenarios. It is hoped that this book will give an overview of banking system to the students and non-financial persons. This will make the banking customers knowledgeable and hence do better banking. For new bankers this will enable them do their operations better with knowledge.

My sincere thanks to Mr. M.P. Sivan Arul, Special Officer, Tamilnadu State Apex Co-operative Bank Ltd., who has written a foreword to this book with pleasantries about the book and the author. Really I am happy that amongst his busy schedules, he could spend his time to read the book entirely and write this foreword.

Definitely thanks are due to the printers and publishers, with whose hard work this book is in this fashion in the hands of the readers.

Please feel free to contact the author for any further details/ comments/ feedback.

Chennai
November 2013

Dr. *Ramamurthy N*

*****

Chapter 1. Globalisation & Monetary Policies

What is Globalisation? – The main cause of globalisation is influence from other, more developed, countries. And the result is removing the geographical barriers. Globalisation is a series of social, economic, technological, cultural, and political changes that promote interdependence and growth. Globalisation raises the standard of living in developing countries, spreads technological knowledge, and increases political liberation. Globalisation is a historical process that results from human innovation and technological progress. The social effects of globalisation are clearly illustrated in Peru and India. Once a third world country filled with poverty and oppression, Peru is now transitioning into a developed nation. In Peru, globalisation has raised the human development index, empowered women, and created a stronger country.

1.1. Peru as on example:

One of the benefits of globalisation on a social level is an increased Human Development Index. The Human Development Index (HDI) is a measurement of a country's social, political, and economic growth in comparison to other countries in the world. The Human Development Index rates each country with a score between 0 and 1, with 1 being the most advanced, globalized country. Factors that are involved in determining a country's HDI are gross domestic production per capita, life expectancy at birth, adult literary, and the number of persons enrolled in educational institutions. In 1975, Peru's Human Development Index was a 0.643. By 2003, the Human Development Index had risen more than one tenth to 0.762. The substantial increase of Peru's HDI is a clear indication that globalisation has made a positive impact. From 1975 until 2003, globalisation has caused a 2% increase in the adult literacy rate. During the same time period, the poverty rate dropped to 6%. Women's fertility rates have also dropped. In 1975, women had an average of 6 children each. In 2003, that average dropped to less than 3 children per woman. When fertility rates drop in developing countries, such as Peru, it is usually an indication that there is an increase in women's liberation. Women are no longer facing as much social pressure to have lots of children and stay home to raise them. By having fewer children, women are exposed to more opportunities for employment. The role of women as housewives and domestic servants is rapidly changing. Women in Peru have begun to experience liberation and equality, mostly due to the spread of globalisation.

1.2. Indian Banking System

The banking system in India is significantly different from that of other Asian nations because of the country's unique geographic, social, and economic characteristics. India has a large population and land size, a diverse culture and extreme disparities in income, which are marked among its regions. There are high levels of illiteracy among a large percentage of population but, at the same time, the country has a large reservoir of managerial and technologically advanced talents. Between about 30 and 35 percent of the population resides in metro and urban cities and the rest is spread in several semi-urban and rural centers.

The country's economic policy framework combines socialistic and capitalistic features with a heavy bias towards public sector investment. India has followed the path of growth-led exports rather than the "export-led growth" of other Asian economies, with emphasis on self-reliance through import substitution. These features are reflected in the structure, size, and diversity of the country's banking and financial sector. The banking system has had to serve the goals of economic policies enunciated in successive five year development plans, particularly concerning equitable income distribution, balanced regional economic growth and the reduction and elimination of private sector monopolies in trade and industry. In order for the banking industry to serve as an instrument of state policy, it was subjected to various nationalisation schemes in different phases (1955, 1969 and 1980). As a result, banking remained internationally isolated (few Indian banks had presence abroad in international financial centers) because of pre-occupations with domestic priorities, especially massive branch expansion and attracting more people to the system. Moreover, the sector has been assigned the role of providing support to other economic sectors such as agriculture, small-scale industries, exports and banking activities in the developed commercial centers.

A big challenge facing Indian banks is how, under the current ownership structure, to attain operational efficiency suitable for modern financial intermediation. On the other hand, it has been relatively easy for the public sector banks to recapitalise, given the increases in non-performing assets

(NPAs), as their Government dominated ownership structure has reduced the conflicts of interest that private banks would face.

1.3. Supervision

Greater transparency in banks' balance sheets and penal action by RBI, including against bank auditors, has resulted in effective monitoring of India's Banking system. Even the 2007 economic crisis, which turned around the globe, did not much affect the Indian economy, more so Indian Banking system. Internal audits in banks, now supervised by audit committees of respective boards, have been resulted in reflecting management's reporting responsibility to the stockholders
of the banks. High standards of preventive and detective (internal) controls are available in banks. However there is more room for improvement. Risk management with respect to "off-balance sheet items" requires considerable attention as evidenced by instances of losses on letters of credits and guarantees business. At the macro level, the size of NPAs as a percentage of GDP provides a good measure to assess the soundness of the system.

1.4. Maturity Mismatch

For a typical bank, Deposits are Liabilities and Loans are Assets. Deposits repaid on the due dates are outflow and the Loans amounts recovered are inflow. While the total of Assets and Liabilities will tally in a balance sheet, the maturity period of deposits and loans may not be the same. Hence arises the maturity mismatch. Matching the inflow and outflow in different time periods is a mammoth task and is called as Asset Liability Management (ALM).

Interest rates have changed several times over the past seven years causing maturity transformations in assets and liabilities and their frequent reprising. A clear and continuous statement of rate sensitive assets and rate sensitive liabilities has to form the basis of interest rate risk management. Central Bank of the country is expected to issue guidelines that show that management-driven Asset Liability Management (ALM) initiatives in banks. This is also the reason why India's money market has remained mostly as a call money market that is meant for clearing day to day temporary surpluses and deficits among banks. Traditionally, many banks, including the foreign banks, have used 'call' money as a regular funding source. PSBs are notably absent players in the market for term funds since they lack data on maturity gaps and interest rate gaps to be complied under ALM discipline. The common complaints about difficulties in collection of data from hundreds of rural and semi urban branches will not be combated unless there is computerisation in these branches to facilitate data compilation progressively (which is not almost achieved). According to RBI and many PSBs, about 80 percent of deposits are term deposits (one to three years). Long-term lending (three to five years) comprises about 30 percent of total loans and thus, maturity mismatch is not a serious issue. However, this claim may not be valid as maturity of deposits and term loans are not disclosed. Moreover, banks have invested a large portion of funds in Government securities and debentures (long-term assets). RBI should highlight and address the real maturity mismatch issue. The 'call' segment of the market is different from the 'term' segment in all sophisticated market centers in the world.

1.5. Bank Computerisation

Entry of new private sector banks and foreign banks offering most modern banking technology has forced PSBs to address computerisation problems more seriously in recent years. The pace of
computerisation has remained slow even though opposition from staff unions has softened. The Central Vigilance Commission wants 100 percent computerisation in Indian banks to check frauds, delays, etc. The general perception is that in recent years, the prime focus of bank computerisation has been less on the number of branches computerized but more on better connectivity, say, between the head office and regional offices of a bank with select branches.

These are usually banks that handle large corporate borrowing accounts on one side and those that are in high deposit zones, on the other. While the private sector banks have been upgrading technology simultaneously with branch expansion, many of the top PSBs have completed automating their branches in the urban areas. The next step to total branch automation is networking these branches. PSBs need to frame a strategy to choose the branches that have to be included in their networking scheme. Since it would be a daunting task for them to connect all the 65+ thousands of branches spread across the country, as a first step, they are following the 80-20 thumb rule. It assumes that 80 percent of bank's business is carried out by only 20 percent of its branches. It is the branches with substantial business, most of which lie in the urban areas, that are initially targeted for interconnection.

A major problem PSBs have to face once IT implementation reaches its optimum level is staff retention. While the private sector banks have been recruiting trained and experienced IT professionals, it may not be possible for PSBs to do likewise. They will have to train their existing staff to function effectively in the new environment. And once the requisite skills are acquired by employees, they may have trouble retaining staff. PSBs can only allocate limited capital resources to computerisation. They will have to choose between high cost of computerisation at metro and urban centers and low cost computerisation at rural, semi-urban branches. Also, they will have to factor in returns on IT assets, and growth and productivity improvements.

1.6. Operational Efficiency

The private sector's partial ownership of SBI has contributed to its exceptional operational efficiency even after 1955 when RBI acquired majority shares. This suggests that it is advisable in the long term for the Indian banking sector to increase the share of private ownership.

In order to reduce the social burden caused by banking sector inefficiency, banks should be given wider management autonomy. The Government should gradually but steadily reduce its ownership of the banking industry while maintaining rigorous prudential regulation and rationalizing its supervision capacity. To bring about efficiency in banks, many a committee was formed and number of measures has been recommended. These included revision and regular update of operational manuals, simplification of documentation systems, introduction of computer audits, and evolution of a filtering mechanism to reduce concentration of exposures in lending and drawing geographical/ industry/ sectorial exposure norms with the Board's concurrence. Besides, the Committees suggested the assignment of full-time directors in nationalized banks. As outsourcing of services would improve productivity, it recommended that the same be introduced in the fields of building maintenance, cleaning, security, dispatch of mail, computer-related work, etc., subject to relevant laws. It also suggested that the minimum stipulated holdings of the Government/ RBI in the equity of nationalized banks/ SBI be reduced to 33 percent.

With regard to the tenure of a bank's chief executive, the Committee indicated a minimum period of three years. However, a more reasonable length of tenure should not be less than five years. Managers should be given incentives to adapt their managerial structure to new developments in financial technologies and to changes in client demand for financial services. The Government needs to seriously consider an increase in management autonomy in the banking industry, because it is essential to efficient management and the Systems and methods in banks should be improved.

Some of the issues are at the micro level and best achieved if banks internalize the system of self-evaluation under the CAMELS rating model. Banks also need to effectively exploit their networks of branches established in the past at low cost. It is necessary for PSBs to introduce factoring services and also activate a short-term bill financing mechanism, both of which entail utilisation of the branch network for collection of the factored invoices and bills for clients.

1.7. Autonomy and Governance

Autonomy and sound governance are likely to be achieved after privatisation of banks has taken place. The Committee's observation that most banks do not even have updated instruction manuals proves the point. RBI's selection of statutory auditors for banks may seem to conflict with the requirement for sound corporate governance. However, such regulatory intervention will remain useful until banks can fully strengthen their internal systems and procedures, risk management standards, and the required preventive and detective controls. Although the problem of overstaffing is a legacy not easy to get rid of,.it has been halted since later 80s through restrictions in fresh recruitment.

All appointments of chairpersons, managing directors, and executive directors of PSBs and financial institutions should be determined by an appointment board. The Committees felt that there was an urgent need to raise competency levels in PSBs through a lateral induction of talented personnel. It also indicated that the remuneration structure should be flexible and market driven. The Government should quickly take steps to induct shareholder nominees on banks who have risen Money from the public but does not have representation on the boards.

1.8. Chapter Summary

Caution must be applied on universal banking because of the following considerations:

- Disintermediation (i.e., replacement of traditional bank intermediation between savers and borrowers by a capital market process) is only a decade old in India and has badly slowed down due to loss of investor confidence;
- There is ample room for financial deepening (by banks and DFIs) since loans market will continue to grow;
- DFIs are now only moving into working capital finance, an area in which they need to gain a lot of experience and this involves creation of a network of services (including branches) in all fields: remittances, collections, etc.; and
- Reforms of India's capital market are still at the halfway stage. The priority will be to ensure branch expansion, financial deepening of the Credit markets, and creation of an efficient credit delivery mechanism that can compete with the capital market.

*****

Chapter 2. Retail vs. Corporate Banking

Retail Banking is services offered to the general public. **Retail banking** is banking in which banking institutions execute transactions directly with consumers, rather than corporations or other banks. Services offered include: savings and transactional accounts, mortgages, personal loans, debit cards, credit cards, and so forth. In contrast with **Wholesale Banking** or corporate banking or commercial Banking, retail banking is a high volume business with many service providers competing for market share. Some retail banking services, for example, credit cards, are among the most profitable services offered by financial institutions.

Wholesale Banking is services offered to corporations with sound financial statements and institutional customers, such as pension funds and government agencies. Services include lending, cash management, commercial mortgages, working capital loans, leasing, trust services, and so on. Most banks divide wholesale banking into several different businesses: the Fortune 500 and Fortune 1000 market, composed of the 500 and 1,000 largest U.S. Corporations, respectively; the Middle Market; and the small business market. Retail Banking services are also termed as Personal Banking services.

In general, opposite of Retail Banking can be taken as Wholesale Banking. This is also called as **Corporate Banking**.

Commercial banks, responding to increased market competition from alternative financing sources, such as commercial paper and junk bonds, have begun to place more emphasis on fee-based corporate services, including foreign exchange and securities trading, advisory services in corporate mergers, and acquisitions, merchant banking, corporate cash management, and securities underwriting.

2.1. Types of Banks

Different types of banks including different meanings are introduced below:

- Commercial bank is the term used for a normal bank to distinguish it from an investment bank. Commercial bank can also refer to a bank or a division of a bank that mostly deals with deposits and loans from corporations or large businesses, as opposed to normal individual members of the public (retail banking).
- Community development bank are regulated banks that provide financial services and credit to underserved markets or populations.
- Private banks manage the assets of high net worth individuals.
- Offshore banks are banks located in jurisdictions with low taxation and regulation. Many offshore banks are essentially private banks.

2.2. Manual vs. Automated Banking

The present day banking has turned as "Click Banking" from "Brick Banking". During manual banking days bankers used to struggle with the routine Day Book, General Ledger, Balance Sheet, Tallying individual ledgers with General Ledger, Interest Applications on loans and deposits, etc. Every half year closing used to be a grand mela for the bankers. This has consumed lot of human efforts. The time allotted by them for business development was very less. At times the bankers used to spend the whole night for finding out a difference of ₹0.10!! If allowed they could have put it from their pocket rather than spending the midnight oil!!

Now all these mundane and routine accounting process and tallying the ledgers are taken care by the systems and the valuable time of the human resource, is available for the core business of the bank. This is reflected in per employee business of the banks.

After the advent of Core Banking Systems, there are no bankers available in banks – in fact they don't need. All the employees have turned out to be Relationship Managers, Marketing Staff and at times computer operators. In a lighter way – if the present employees are asked "How to calculate interest on pre-closure of Fixed Deposit" they would reply "Press F3". Earlier banking industry itself was used to be called as Service Industry – servicing to the clients. Now everything is productised and hence banking industry does not have clients, but only have customers.

Also on account of Core Banking System the "Branch Banking" has manifested into "Bank Banking".

At the same time, the processes used in manual systems were defined and being in use for centuries. Due to Core Banking System the processes have to be re-engineered – giving a different dimension to frauds – i.e. e-fraud or IT-frauds. The frauds in banking industry used to be called as "White collar fraud" and now it has become all the more easy – by sitting in one place and attacking the entire globe.

In a way the security threats are multi-dimensional and hence the protection forces also should be well-equipped towards the same.

On the other hand, earlier banks used to have kilos of papers of accounts in ledgers. Now the accounts, the transactions, etc., are wealth of Data for the banks. They could very well be analysed and used to customize the products to the specific needs of that particular zone or area.

To summarize – the definition of Retail Banking can be taken as dealing with individual customers while Corporate Banking deal with business customers – whether it is lending or accepting deposits. It is very clear that the focus of the entire banking industry and its security has drastically changed and continue to change.

*****

Chapter 3. Working Capital

Working Capital refers to that part of the firm's capital, which is required for financing short-term or current assets such as cash, marketable securities, debtors and inventories. Funds thus, invested in current assets keep revolving fast and are constantly converted into cash and this cash flow out again in exchange for other current assets. To assess or even to define the working capital it is mandatory to understand about corporates and their financial statements.

What is a corporate? - A corporate has a special entity – not enjoyed by Partnership neither by Sole Proprietorship firms. These are denoted, in different countries as: –

- Ltd. (Limited)
- Private [(P), (Pvt)] Ltd. (Private Limited)
- LLC – (Limited Liability Company)
- Inc. – (Incorporated)
- LLP – (Limited Liability Partnership)
- Government Corporations
- Municipalities

The Certificate of Incorporation given by the Registrar of Companies is the birth certificate for the corporate. An account can be opened in the name of a corporate, only if there is a resolution to that effect by the concerned board. Operations in the account should be by those officials authorised in that regard by the board. Besides, any borrowing by a company needs specific approval from the company's board. Similarly, even account closing should be only as per a board resolution.

However, for the limited purpose of this book – to deal with corporate banking – the connotation of the term corporate is expanded to include Sole Proprietorship and Partnership firms also. It should be read to denote a firm and not the legal term of corporate defined above.

3.1. Financial Statements

The financial position and performance of a firm is understood through various financial statements. The major financial statements are:

- Trading Account – wherever applicable
- Manufacturing Account – wherever applicable
- Profit and Loss Statement
- Balance Sheet
- Cash Flow statement
- Funds Flow statement

Through these statements, the below positions of the firm can be assessed:

- Profitability
- Solvency
- Liquidity
- Repayment capacity

Now, let us dive into the various terms and statements mentioned above:

The **Financial Performance** is defined as – the results of decisions over time. This could be understood through:

- Trading/ Profit & Loss Account during a certain time period (usually, a year) would help the stakeholders to analyse different Income and Expenses incurred during that period. It is also called as Income and Expenses Statement or Receipts & Payments Statement

The **Financial Position** of a firm is defined as – the total resources controlled by a business and the claims against those resources. This could be understood through:

- Balance Sheet as on a certain date by analysing the
    - Assets and Liabilities
    - Also called a Net Worth Statement
- Cash and Funds Flow Statements
    - Flow of cash IN and OUT
    - Non-Cash items IN and OUT

Profit and Loss (P&L) Statement for a period at a high level should reveal:

- Cash Income
- Cash Expenses
- Net Cash Income = Cash income – Cash expenses
- Change in Inventory position

- Depreciation & Capital Adjustments
- Net Income = Net cash income – inventory change – depreciation

A P&L account will have some annexures called Schedules (as per India GAAP there are Schedules I to M to a P&L account). These annexures provide lot of information about the performance of a firm like:

- Basis for preparing the P&L account
- Any change in accounting policies or procedures
- Any one off transaction during the year like sale of fixed assets, etc. (This would be detailed in one of the Schedules attached to P&L statement)
- Inventory position, sales return, purchase return, etc.
- Transactions relating to Directors and their close relatives
- Related party disclosures and so on.

A company's **Balance Sheet** as on a particular date at a high level – will look like:

Liabilities		**Assets**	
Capital		Current	
Reserves & Surplus		Fixed	
Current		Investments	
Term		Others	
Total (TL)		Total (TA)	
Net Worth (NW) = Capital + Reserves & Surplus			

Current Assets include:

- Cash, near-cash, or items normally used or sold in the course of business during the current financial year
- Cash & Bank Balances
- Short Term investments – maturing within the current financial year
- Supplies, inventories
- Prepaid expenses
- Accounts receivable and so on

Assets which are not **current**:

- Machinery and equipment, breeding livestock
- Investments in Shares and debentures
- Land, buildings, and other improvements to land
- Intermediate assets including machinery
- Long-term investments – maturing later than the current financial year

Current Liabilities include:

- Liabilities due within the current financial year
- Operating loans – Cash Credit, Overdraft, Demand Loan, etc.
- Short term loans
- Accounts payable, accrued interest
- Rents and lease payments due within the current financial year
- That portion of term debt due within the current financial year

Long term liabilities cover

- Liabilities associated with non-current assets
    - Machinery loans and leases
    - Real estate loans and contracts
    - Leases on buildings (e.g., silos)
- Medium & Long Term Loans. Even in these loans the installments due for payment within this current financial year should be treated as current liabilities
- Capital

Similar to Profit & Loss Statement a balance sheet also will have some annexures called Schedules (as per India GAAP there are Schedules A to F to a balance sheet). These annexures provide lot of information about the performance of a firm like:

- Micro level details of the capital
- Any change in capital
- Depreciation methods
- Revaluation of assets
- Any one off transaction during the year like sale of fixed assets, etc.
- Loss and provisions required to be made and made
- And so forth.

Cash and funds flow

- Cash Inflow
  - Product sales
  - Capital sales
- Cash Outflow
  - Expenses, capital purchases, proprietor withdrawals, etc.
  - Term loan payments
- Flow of Funds Summary
  - Beginning cash balance, borrowings & payment of Operating loans, ending cash balance
  - Loan Balances

Objectives of **funds flow** statement

- Basically the funds flow statement would cover the funds generated/ utilised from the primary operation of the firm. For instance profit or loss incurred on account of sale of fixed assets would not be considered in funds flow – since this is one off item and it is not the normal operation of the firm.
- To check whether funds are used for the purpose for which they were raised
- To find out any diversion of funds – short to long term or vice versa

Difference between cash and funds flow statement

- Cash flow is on real cash terms whereas funds flow includes non-cash items like depreciation, good will, etc.
- Cash flow indicates ability to meet current obligations whereas funds flow indicates long term obligations
- Cash flow provides an idea on how fast current assets get converted into cash
- Funds flow checks whether funds raised from various sources are properly utilised and matched
- Cash flow is an indicator of liquidity and solvency

3.2. Financial Ratios

If somebody says that his firm has made profit of ₹ 1 crore, the audience take it as a statement and does not make much of sense to the readers. Instead if it is said the profit is 40% of the capital or 25% of the sales the reader is much informed about the performance of the firm. Also the reader can compare the performance with that of the standard in the region, industry, country, etc. In other words the reader can assess the performance of the firm when he knows the **profitability** of 40% instead of a **profit** of ₹ 1 crore.

Here comes the role of various financial rations revealing in detail about the Profitability, Solvency, Liquidity and Repayment capacity of the firms.

A ratio is the relationship expressed in qualitative terms between figures which have cause and effect relationships or which are connected with each other in some manner or other.

A Ratio is expressed in

- Proportion
- Rate or times or co-efficient
- Percentage

The process of a financial ratio is:

- Selection of relevant information
- Comparison of calculated ratios
- Interpretation and reporting

Advantages and limitations of financial ratios:

- Advantages
  - Better Forecasting
  - Increased Managerial control
  - Quantitative measuring of efficiency
  - Facilitate investment / lending decisions
  - A tool for comparison
- Limitations
  - Requires a high level of Practical knowledge
  - Ratios are only means/ averages and not necessarily need to indicate the actual performance
  - Non-availability of standards or norms
  - Accuracy of financial information

- Consistency in preparation of financial statements – for e.g. if there is a change in method of calculating of depreciation, that would affect the P&L without a change in the production/ sales.
- Change in price level – for e.g. if there is a change in the valuation of assets like fixed assets, investments, etc. the P&L would be affected without a change in the production/ sales.

Various financial ratios can be classified based on its purpose as:

Table 1 – Table of Financial Ratios

#	Purpose/ Function	Ratio	Formula
1.	Profitability	Gross Profit Ratio	Gross Profit / Net Sales
2.		Operating Profit Ratio	Operating Profit / Net Sales
3.		Net Profit Ratio	Net Profit / Net Sales
4.	Turnover	Stock Turnover Ratio	Cost of goods sold / average inventory
5.		Creditors Turnover Ratio	Net Credit purchases / average accounts payable
6.		Debtors Turnover Ratio	Net Credit Sales / Average receivables
7.		Working Capital Ratio	Sales (or) cost of sales / Net working capital
8.		Fixed Assets Ratio	Net Sales/ Net Fixed Assets
9.	Short Term Solvency	Current Ratio	Current Assets / Current Liabilities
10.		Liquidity Ratio	Quick Assets / Current Liabilities
11.		Absolute Liquidity Ratio or Cash Position Ratio	(Cash & Bank balance + marketable securities) / current liabilities
12.	Long Term Solvency	Proprietary Ratio	Shareholder's fund/ total tangible assets
13.		Debt Equity Ratio	Total Debt / Total Tangible assets
14.		Fixed Assets Ratio	As in 8 above
15.		Capital Gearing Ratio	Long term loans + Debentures + preference

#	Purpose/ Function	Ratio	Formula
			capital / Equity shareholders' funds
16.	Balance Sheet	Liquidity Ratio	As in 10 above
17.		Current Ratio	As in 9 above
18.		Debt Equity Ratio	As in 13 above
19.	Profit and Loss	Gross Profit Ratio	As in 1 above
20.		Operating Profit Ratio	As in 2 above
21.		Net Profit Ratio	As in 3 above
22.	Composite	Return on Investment	Operating Profit / Capital employed
23.		Debtor Turnover	As in 6 above
24.		Earnings Per Share	Dividend earned/ value of per share
25.	Management	Operating Profit Ratio	As in 2 above
26.		Creditors Turnover Ratio	As in 5 above
27.		Debtors Turnover Ratio	As in 6 above
28.		Profit Ratios	As in 1 above
29.		Solvency Ratio	Total Debt / Total Tangible assets
30.	Creditors	Debt Service coverage Ratio	Profit BIT / Interest + Principal payment installment / (1 - Tax rate)
31.		Liquidity Ratio	As in 10 above
32.		Debt Equity Ratio	Total Long term debt / shareholders' funds or External equities / internal equities
33.		Solvency Ratio	As in 29 above
34.	Shareholders	Earnings Per Share	As in 24 above

Out of the above ratios Current Ratio and profitability ratios are the ones keenly looked into by all the stakeholders.

The acceptable level for some of the key ratios is:

• Current Ratio	=	1.33 : 1
• Liquidity Ratio	=	1
• Absolute Liquidity Ratio/ Cash Position Ratio	=	0.75 : 1
• Fixed Assets Ratio	=	1
• Debt Equity Ratio	=	1
• Solvency Ratio	=	1
• Proprietary Ratio	=	not < 0.5
• All profit ratios	=	not < 0

3.3. Working Capital

Working capital typically means the firm's holding of current or short term assets such as cash, receivables, inventory and marketable securities. These items are also referred to as revolving or circulating or short-term capital. Corporate executives devote a considerable amount of attention to the management of working capital.

"Circulating capital means current assets of a company that are changed in the ordinary course of business from one form to another, as for example, from cash to inventories, inventories to receivables, receivable to cash"

......Genestenbreg

Globally there are two possible interpretations of Working Capital concept as:

- Balance sheet concept
- Operating cycle concept

3.3.1. Balance Sheet concept of working capital

Again within balance sheet concept there are two interpretations as:

- Excess of current assets over current liabilities
- Gross or total current assets.

Typically in an ideal situation a firm is expected to meet its long term assets with long term liabilities and short term assets with short term liabilities. But this will not be true in reality. Some of the current assets are met by long term liabilities and hence short term liabilities are more than the short term assets.

Ideal situation

Long Term Liabilities	Long Term Assets
Short Term Liabilities	Short Term Assets

Reality

<table>
<tr><td rowspan="2">Long Term Liabilities</td><td>Long Term Assets</td></tr>
<tr><td rowspan="2">Short Term Assets</td></tr>
<tr><td>Short Term Liabilities</td></tr>
</table>

The difference between current liabilities and current assets is called Working Capital Gap or Net Working Capital.

I.e. Working Capital Gap = Current liabilities - Current Assets.

To meet this gap the firms approach banks for working capital finance.

Working capital finance is a part of long term finance used for supporting current activities. The balance sheet definition of working capital is an indication of the firm's current solvency. Shortage of working capital indicates scarcity of cash resources.

3.3.2. Operating cycle concept of working capital

A company's operating cycle typically consists of three primary activities:

- Purchasing resources
- Producing the product and
- Distributing (selling) the product

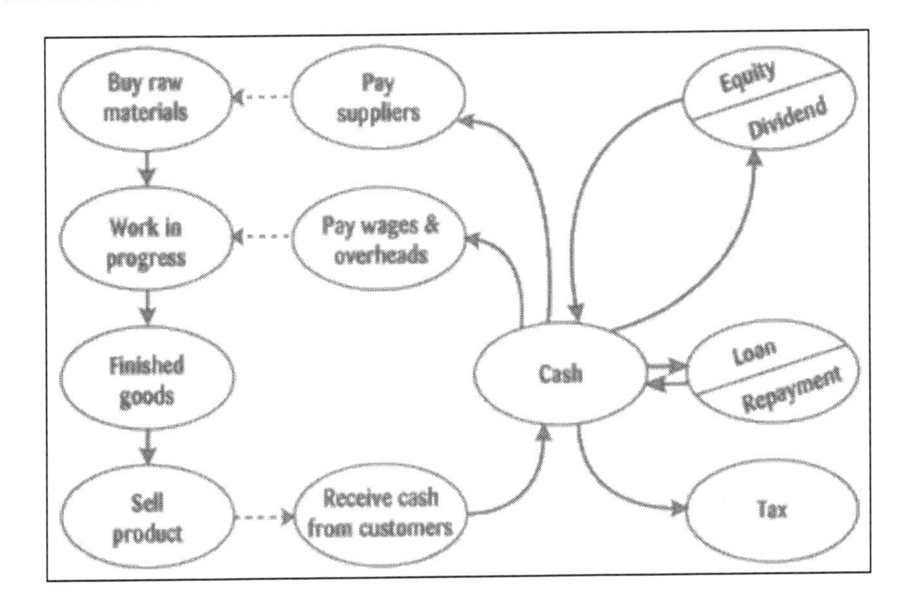

Figure 1 – Operating Cycle

Operating cycle creates **unsynchronised** and **uncertain** funds flow. Unsynchronised cash disbursements take place before cash receipts and it is uncertain because future sales and costs cannot be forecasted accurately. But still the firm has to maintain cash balance to pay the bills as they come due. In addition, the firm must invest in inventories to fill customer orders promptly. And finally, the firm invests in accounts receivable to extend credit to customers. Hence, Operating Cycle can be defined as equal to the length of inventory and receivable conversion periods.

To meet the working capital needs i.e. cash outflows during this operating period, firms need working capital finance.

3.4. Chapter Summary

Through the financial statements of a firm, the financial position of the firm can be assessed and its, Profitability, Solvency, Liquidity and Repayment capacity can also be understood.

The various financial ratios help the banks and other stakeholders to understand performance of the firm more clearly.

The immediate cash needs of a firm are called working capital. This is of different types viz.

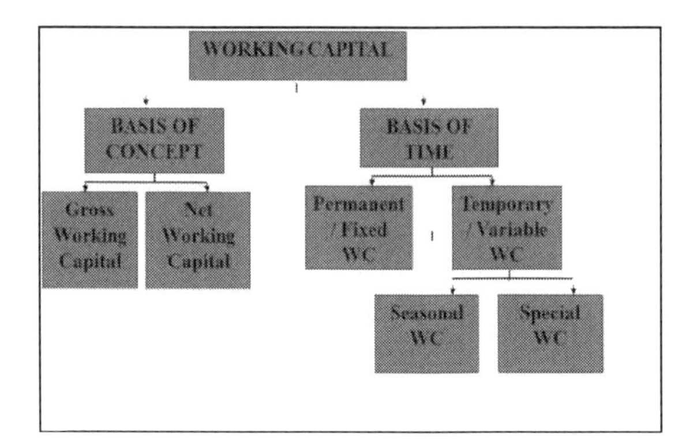

Figure 2 – Types of Working Capital Finance

The excess of the current liabilities over the current assets is called Working Capital Gap and to meet this gap, firms approach banks for working capital finance.

Banks do offer various corporate products to cater to the working capital needs of the firms.

The different products and the appraisal methods followed by the banks are discussed in next chapters.

*****

Chapter 4. Corporate Banking Products

To meet the working capital gap/ needs of the corporates different banks offer different products customised to the local needs of the customers/ regions.

Whatever be the product it will fall under one of the two major classifications viz.

- Funded Finance
- Non-funded Finance

4.1. Some Credit Concepts

Some of the credit jargons/ concepts are explained below. This will enable clear understanding of the types of credit, appraisal process, etc.

4.1.1. Credit Scoring

Regardless of whether the appraisal process is manual or mechanised, in the retail front, most banks use a framework by name "Credit Scoring" to evaluate individual proposals. Under this, marks are assigned to various parameters/ attributes that find a place in the proposal. And using varying weights for different parameters, an aggregate score, otherwise called "Credit Score" is arrived at for individual borrowers. If the Credit Score is more than the minimum threshold acceptable, the proposal is sanctioned. Conversely, if the Credit Score for a particular borrower is less than the minimum threshold, then the proposal stands rejected.

4.1.2. Interest Rate

In respect of loans, there are quite a many way of charging interest. Some of methods highly in vogue universally are:

- Fixed
- Floating
- Cap
- Floor
- Collar

Fixed Rate of Interest – In the case of fixed rate contract, the rate of interest payable by the borrower would remain the same throughout the tenure of the loan regardless of what happens to the general market interest rates. By locking to a fixed rate, for sure, the borrower is protecting himself/ herself from the adverse impact of any upward revision in the market rates. But, at the same time, he/ she also has to forgo the benefit that could have accrued to him/ her during moments of interest rate fall/ crash.

Floating Rate of Interest – Sometimes, the bank and/ or the borrower may like to have a floating rate of interest. In such cases, they need to agree on three things. First of all, they should agree on the "benchmark rate"— also called "base rate" or "anchor rate" – with reference to which the interest rate payable by the borrower would float. Such a benchmark rate should be a commonly accepted one. (For instance, it can be LIBOR or SIBOR or MIBOR or PLR of the bank or the Treasury-bill rate. Sometimes, banks may use their own Term Deposit rate as the benchmark rate).

Having fixed the benchmark rate, the bank decides the add-on to the benchmark rate for arriving at the actual rate payable by the borrower. Besides, there is one more thing to be agreed upon. That is the frequency with which the interest rate payable by the borrower would be reset.

Cap – this is a floating rate of interest with a maximum limit fixed, while sanctioning the loan itself, more than which the rate of interest cannot move. This is in a way advantageous to the borrower.

Floor – this is a floating rate of interest with a minimum limit fixed, while sanctioning the loan itself, less than which the rate of interest cannot move. This is in a way advantageous to the bank.

Collar – this is a floating rate of interest with minimum and maximum limits fixed, while sanctioning the loan itself, less or more than which the rate of interest cannot move. This protects the interest of both the bank and the borrower.

4.1.3. Repayment Methods

As is the case with rate of interest methods, there is many a way, in which the repayment can be structured. Some of them are;

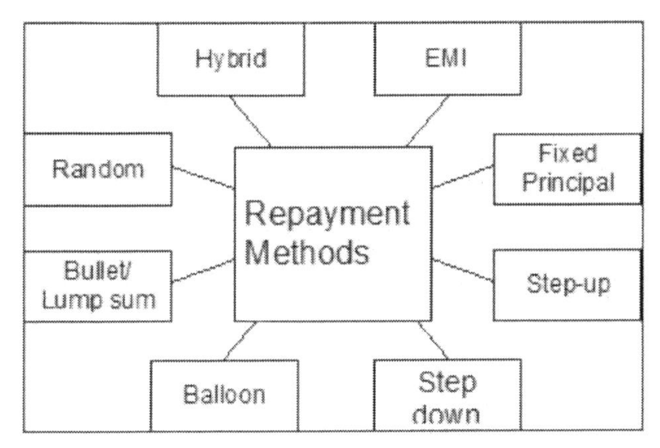

Figure 3 – Repayment Methods

Every method has its own advantages and disadvantages. Whenever the borrower is given the option, he/ she should select the one that suits his/ her present and future cash inflows, other commitments as well as the tax consequences.

Equated Monthly Installment (EMI) – In the case of EMI, for a given principal, RoI and tenor of the loan, the monthly repayment quantum remains constant throughout the period of the loan. With each installment, what changes is the respective proportion of principal and interest. The proportion of interest in the total installment quantum comes down with each installment. Inversely, the proportion of principal component goes up.

Fixed Principal – As the name indicates, what is kept constant in this method is the amount of principal payable during each installment. The interest portion would keep varying. Everything else remaining the same, the absolute quantum of interest component would keep coming down with every installment. Naturally, this implies, the total installment commitment would taper off over time.

Step-up – Under the step-up repayment model, in general the total commitment (interest + principal) gets stepped up in stages. Suppose 'X' is the amount of the first six installments. And from the 7th to 12th installment, the amount is stepped upto '1.2X'. And again from the 13th to 18th installment the commitment gets stepped upto '1.5X' and so on. Step-up model is advantages for those customers who are expecting a steady rise in their disposable income at fixed intervals.

Step-down – This is an exact mirror Image of the step-up method. Here the total commitment is initially set at a higher level. After a certain number of installments, it is brought down by a factor. And again after an equal number of further installments, it is brought down further.

Balloon – This is a very special repayment pattern, not often used in the retail segment. It is more prevalent in corporate banking. Under this, the borrower and the banker agree on the total period within which the loan would be cleared in full. And the borrower keeps paying a notional amount every time till the last installment. The last payment would generally be very huge in comparison to other installments. Balloon type installment scheme is ideal when the borrower is expecting a windfall at the fag end of the repayment period and is not in a position to meet sizeable repayment commitments at present. In some places this method is a blend of step-up and step-down methods. The repayment gradually increases and after some time it decreases.

Bullet/ Lump Sum – Under this method, the borrower gets a certain time for repaying the loan. Till the due date, he/ she keeps paying only the interest portion. And on the final due date, he/she repays the entire principal amount in one shot. Or again the borrower has the right to repay the principal in parts at any point of time during the tenor of the loan. However, he has to repay the interest as and when charged.

Random – As the very name makes it obvious, the repayment pattern is random. Such randomness can relate to two factors: the date/ dates on which various installments would be paid and/ or the quantum, of each such installment. Under this method, the borrower repays whatever amount he/ she can and whenever he can. Such a repayment structure is extremely advantageous to the borrower, but can make life tough for the bank.

Hybrid – Occasionally a customer may like to follow a repayment pattern that is a hybrid of any two or more of the methods above. In such situations, banks tailor the repayment schedule to suit his/ her convenience. Such a structure, he/ she may think, may be in tandem with his/ her expected future cash inflows.

It can be noted that at present, all the methods discussed above may not be available in a single country. It is a list of global methods.

4.1.4. Security and Charge Types

While banks may occasionally extend credit sans-security, more often than not they get their lending secured in one way or the other. Such a security can be the very asset being financed by the loan or something else in addition. In the lexicon of some of the banks, when the financed asset itself becomes a security for the loan given, it is called "Primary Security". On the other hand, when an asset that is not financed by the loan becomes an additional security for the loan given, it is christened 'collateral' or "Secondary Security". However, in some of the western banks' context, the term collateral stands for any asset offered as security to the lender.

Charge Type – Security cannot be homogeneous in nature. Depending upon the type of loan being sanctioned, anything from shares to house property to life insurance policy can be offered as security. As the nature of these securities differs, so does the method of establishing the financing banks' rights over them. The following are the generic ways in which banks establish their rights over the securities offered to them.

Pledge – Possibly one of the most common place methods of establishing charge. When an asset is pledged in favour of a bank, the latter would have its physical possession. This automatically rules out the usage of the asset by the borrower during the currency of the loan. In the retail banking domain, pledge is used in respect of assets such as gold, etc. In case the borrower defaults, under pledge, the bank would have the automatic right to dispose of the asset and use the sale proceeds for wiping off the dues in the borrower's loan account. At the same time, the bank is duty bound to pay to the borrower any sale proceeds received in excess of the loan outstanding. In the case of pledge the possession is with the lender and the ownership lies with the borrower.

Hypothecation – From a legal point of view, hypothecation is as good as pledge. The only difference is in this case the borrower can retain the possession of the asset and use it. In retail banking, vehicles financed stand hypothecated to the bank, not pledged to it. For, if the funded vehicles were to be pledged, borrower cannot use it till he/ she pays the last installment. In the case of hypothecation the possession lies with the borrower and the ownership lies with the lender.

Lien – Banks use lien as a method of establishing their charge in respect of those assets/ valuables that come to their possession in the natural course of their business. This is applicable to the securities like Fixed Deposits of banks or other corporates, shares, etc.

Assignment – Assignment is a process by which the beneficial rights of one person over an asset (claim/ receivable/ contract) get transferred to another. This method of charge is applicable in the case of Life Insurance Policies being offered as security.

Mortgage – Mortgage is always applicable for immovable properties being offered as security. In general, transfer of title/ interest in any immovable property from one person to another is affected by putting through mortgage. Mortgage has a lot of variants within it. In fact, in some of the variants, no actual transfer of title happens at all except in case of need. Of the different variants of mortgages, two are most common:

Registered Mortgage and **Mortgage by deposit of title deeds** – also called as Equitable Mortgage. Under registered mortgage there is an actual transfer of title from one person to another. On the other hand, when an equitable mortgage transaction is put through, there is no actual transfer at that moment, only an explicit consent by the property owner to handover over the title deed as a security[1].

4.1.5. Technical Terms of Credit

Understanding some technical terms like Limit, Margin, Drawing Power, Liability, Excess Drawing, etc., will enable a clear appreciation of further topics discussed.

Instead of defining the concepts, it is better understood through an example.

A borrower approaches his banker for a car loan – to purchase a car, which costs ₹6,00,000/-.

Even if the borrower is otherwise eligible for a loan of ₹6,00,000/-, the bank may not lend the entire cost of the car. The borrower has to meet some portion of it say 25% viz. ₹1,50,000/-. This amount is called **margin** amount.

---

[1] Mortgage as a type of loan discussed later in the same chapter

The bank sanctions the remaining amount of ₹4,50,000/-. This is the **limit** of the loan beyond which the outstanding cannot go at any point of time. The EMI has been fixed at ₹20,000/- per month.

After two years – the borrower would have paid ₹2,40,000/- and a sum of ₹1,50,000/- has been added as interest. Hence the loan outstanding is:

As on 01st January 2010 – loan sanctioned	₹4,50,000/- (1)
As on 01st January 2012 – add interest charged so far	₹1,50,000/- (2)
Less repayments	₹2,40,000/- (3)
Amount **outstanding** (1) + (2) – (3)	₹3,60,000/-

This amount of ₹3,60,000/- is the **drawing power** or **liability** of the borrower as on 01st January 2012. In this case the liability and the drawing power are equal.

Assuming during these two years, the borrower has repaid only ₹1,40,000/. The liability would be ₹4,60,000/-. But the drawing power remains the same as ₹3,60,000/-. Hence there is an **excess** or **above the limit** of ₹1,00,000/-. (In practice, if there are dues in repayments, the interest charged would be higher. For simplifying the calculations the interest charged is retained as it is.)

In the first place, a bank fixes the eligible limit for the borrower. This is the maximum permissible outstanding in the account at any point of time. Besides, the bank would also impose a margin requirement (say, 30%) *vis-à-vis* whatever asset that is offered as security for the loan.

In the case of loan accounts, which are meant as running accounts, the maximum permissible outstanding is either the limit or the value of asset/ security minus the margin portion *called drawing power* - whichever is less. Under no circumstances, can the drawing power exceed the limit sanctioned to the borrower. Often, the drawing power keeps varying at very frequent intervals when the borrowing is against certain types of assets like equity shares. On the other hand, the limit remains stable for a fairly long period of time, and only occasionally it is revised either upwards or downwards.

4.2. Funded Finance

Various types of funded finance are offered to customers by different banks.

4.2.1. Cash Credit

In general there are two types of cash credit accounts.

- Open Cash Credit (OCC)
- Key Cash Credit (KCC)

Cash credit may be given against:

- Pledge or hypothecation of goods or produce or documents of title thereto,
- Demand promissory notes, secured by:
  - Hypothecation of stocks of goods or produce (sometimes supported by hypothecation of other assets),
  - Debentures or fully paid shares of limited liability companies
  - Immovable property or documents of title thereto;
  - Hypothecation of book debts and other assets.

4.2.1.1. Open Cash Credit

OCC is an operating account through which a borrower can withdraw funds as and when needed up to the credit limit already sanctioned by the banker. Under this, the borrower can repay the amount anytime, and interest will be charged on amount borrowed and not on the credit limit sanctioned by the bank to the borrower.

This form of borrowing is extremely useful to the borrower because under this method borrower can draw the amount as and when required by and also he has to pay only interest on the amount which he has withdrawn and not on the full amount and thereby providing flexibility to the borrower.

Features of an Open Cash Credit Account are:

- Operative account - Account is operated in exactly same manner as a current account

- A drawing account against the limit sanctioned by the bank
- Advance is secured by hypothecation of goods – raw materials, work in progress and finished goods
- Accounts should not be overdrawn beyond the drawing power (DP) or the limit, whichever is lower. DP is calculated based on the value of goods hypothecated after adjusting the accepted margin.
- Interest should be served as and when it is due
- Normally sanctioned for 1 year and renewed on satisfactory operations.
- The operations are reviewed periodically with stock statements and other financial statements.

4.2.1.2. Key Cash Credit (KCC)

KCC is also similar to OCC while in operation there are a few differences which are:

- OCC is against hypothecation of goods. Possession of the goods is with the borrower.
- KCC is against pledge of goods. Possession of the goods is with the bank.
- OCC is a running account and KCC is a kind of loan account. Amount is disbursed depending on the value of goods pledged with the bank

On account of various operational in-convenience and legal formalities in maintaining the pledged goods, banks do not encourage KCC facility.

4.2.2. Overdraft

Overdraft facility is almost operationally similar to OCC. Overdrafts may be granted against:

- Government or other securities
- Debentures or other securities of certain district boards, municipalities, port trusts and improvement trusts etc.
- Debentures and fully paid shares
- The Bank's own deposits
- The surrender value of life insurance policies
- Other securities NSCs, Bonds etc.

4.2.3. Demand Loan

A Demand Loan is a term loan and not an operative account like OCC. Demand loans are granted against:

- Any of the types of security enumerated under 'Overdrafts'
- Pledge of gold ornaments
- Pledge of other goods or produce or documents (including warehouse receipt)
- Debentures or fully paid shares of limited liability companies
- Immovable property or documents
- Units of mutual funds

Features of a Demand Loan are:

- A demand loan account is an advance for a fixed amount
- Not an operative account.
- No debits may be made subsequent to the initial advance except for interest, insurance and other sundry charges.

4.2.4. Term Loan

Features of Term Loans:

- A term loan is an advance, usually against security of the borrowers' fixed assets, for a fixed period to a business or an industrial undertaking
- A term loan may be granted for the purpose of acquisition of fixed assets, viz., land, buildings, plant and machinery, etc., for setting up new industrial units or expansion or modernisation of existing undertakings.
- Re-payment period up to one year will be termed as short-term loans (STLs), while loans with maturity exceeding one year but up to three years will be termed as medium term loans (MTLs) and those with longer maturity will be known as long term loans or simply term loans (TLs).

4.3. Bill Facility

Normally, if the working capital need of a company is more than a threshold amount say ₹ 1 crore, generally one-third of the limit is sanctioned as bill facility. The bill facility is of different types like:

- Purchase
- Supply
- Negotiation

This has been dealt with in detail under Trade Finance chapter.

4.4. Project Finance:

A project can be defined as:

- **Projects have a purpose**: Projects have clearly-defined aims and set out to produce clearly-defined results. Their purpose is to solve a 'problem', and this involves analysing needs beforehand. Suggesting one or more solutions, it aims at lasting social change.
- **Projects are realistic**: Their aims must be achievable, and this means taking into account both requirements and the financial and human resources available.
- **Projects are limited in time and space**: They have a beginning and an end, and are implemented in a specific place and context.
- **Projects are complex**: Projects call on various planning and implementation skills, and involve various partners and players.
- **Projects are collective**: Projects are the product of collective endeavour. They are run by teams, involve various partners and cater for the needs of others.
- **Projects are unique:** All projects stem from new ideas. They provide a specific response to a need (problem) in a specific context. They are innovative.
- **Projects are an adventure**: Every project is different and ground-breaking; they always involve some uncertainty and risk.
- **Projects can be assessed**: Projects are planned and broken down into measurable aims, which must be open to evaluation.
- **Projects are made up of stages**: Projects have distinct, identifiable stages.

A project Appraisal:

- Is a generic term that refers to the process of assessing, in a structured way, the case for proceeding with a project or proposal. In short, project appraisal is the effort of calculating a project's **viability**.

- Involves a collection of instruments that can be used to determine the **financial** viability (such as the internal rates of return, etc.)

In general, project finance covers:

- Green field industrial projects, capacity expansion at existing manufacturing units, construction ventures or other infrastructure projects.
- Capital intensive business expansion and diversification as well as replacement of equipment may be financed through the project term loans.
- The loans are approved on the basis of strong in-house appraisal of the cost and viability of the ventures as well as the credit standing of promoters.

4.5. Non-Funded Finance

In addition to various types of funded facilities offered by banks, the corporate customers also need some non-funded facilities like:

- Letter of Credit (LC)

    - A documentary credit – an undertaking issued by a bank
    - On behalf of the buyer (the importer)
    - To the seller (exporter)
    - To pay for goods and services
    - Provided that the seller presents documents which comply with the terms and conditions of the documentary credit.

- Bank Guarantee (BG)

    - A contract of guarantee is defined as "a contract to perform the promise or discharge the liability of a third person in case of default".
    - The parties to the contract of guarantee are:
        - Applicant: The principal debtor – person at whose request the guarantee is executed
        - Beneficiary: Person to whom the guarantee is given and who can enforce it in case of default.
        - Guarantor: The person who undertakes to discharge the obligations of the applicant in case of his default.

Banks may issue guarantees generally for the following purposes:

- In lieu of security deposit/earnest money deposits for participating in tenders;
- In respect of raw material supplies or for advances by the buyers;
- In respect of due performance of specific contracts by the borrowers and for obtaining full payment of the bills;
- To allow units to draw funds from time to time from the concerned indenters against part execution of contracts, etc.

In the case of non-funded finance:

- Banks do not have to lay out funds immediately and hence it is called as non-fund based finance.
- Commitments there under contain inherent risks
- If the customers do not meet the related obligations when due, the Bank has to meet them and the concerned commitments would turn into fund-based exposures. Hence it is called as contingent liability for the banks.

4.6. Export-Import loans

There are different types of export import loan needs for corporates. The major classifications are:

- Post Shipment Finance
- Packing Credit

These are discussed in detail under Trade Finance chapter.

4.7. Loan Syndication

When more than one bank or Financial Institution join together in lending to borrower for a particular purpose, it is called Loan Syndication. One of the banks or FIs is called leader of the consortium. This is generally to assemble large loan packages involving a chain of reputed financial entities, domestic and international, that matches the large credit requirements of infrastructure projects.

4.8. Chapter Summary

Banks do offer different types of finance to corporates like

- Term Loan
- Demand Loan
- Cash Credit – Open cash credit and Key cash credit
- Bill finance
- Export-Import finance

If it is a new project, banks do consider it under project finance.

More than one bank or FI join together as a Syndicate, to lend for a particular corporate and for a particular purpose.

*****

Chapter 5. Credit Appraisal

It is a topic of ongoing and never ending debate – whether Credit Appraisal is an 'Art' or 'Science'? If it is a science it will fit into some logic and hence can completely be automated. If it is an art no system can support it. It is a blend of both. It is an art – interview of the prospective borrower by the bankers is a must to assess the capability and intent of the loan applicants. However, it has to be supported by various projected financial statements, ratios, etc., which systems can only support with accurate calculations.

5.1. Trends in Corporate Finance

During the period – later 70s and early 80s – mainly in India, the funds available for lending with banks were in scarcity. Banks wanted to restrict lending including working capital finance. Borrowers used to wait out of the office of the officials of the banks for appointment. The borrowers were ready to pay any rate of interest charged by the banks. But the scene has changed entirely. The officials from banks have started waiting out of the office of CxOs, mainly CFOs of worthy prospective borrowers. Also the banks are ready to offer special pricing viz., reduced rate of interest for these types of borrowers, since banks do have lot of funds and want to lend to the worthy and needy borrowers. However, the focus is on securities/ collaterals – since under Basel norms banks need to maintain proportional capital if the credit is not backed by appropriate securities.

That is, the trend is keeping on changing depending on the regulations, availability of funds, etc.

5.2. Array of appraisals

When anyone talks about credit appraisal, immediately he is tempted to think of different financial statements and ratios. This forms part of Financial Appraisal. But the financial appraisal is fourth in priority. There are many more areas to be considered before even considering financial statements. The entire gamut of credit appraisal can be segregated as:

- External Analysis – (PEST) analysis
    - Political
    - Economic
    - Social

    - Technological
- Industrial Analysis
- Internal Analysis
    - Organisation
    - Promoters
    - Business
    - 4 P's-Product, Place, Price & Promotion, People,
    - Strategy – Sales and Marketing, Production Process etc.

This in turn can be regrouped as:

- Borrower Appraisal
- Technical Appraisal
- Management Appraisal
- Financial Appraisal
- Market Appraisal
- Economic Appraisal
- Environmental Appraisal

5.2.1. Borrower Appraisal

Among different types of appraisals noted above, the borrower appraisal is top most. This would reveal the capability of the borrower to repay the loan. More than capability his willingness or mindset to repay the loan is more important. Even if he has capability, if he is not willing to repay, the loan will never be repaid. On the other hand, if he has mindset to repay, even if he is not presently capable, he will somehow work hard, earn and repay the loan. Hence to assess a borrower, the Five Cs – as discussed below are assessed.

5.2.1.1. Five 'C's of the borrower

Confidence is the basis of all credit transactions. This is the cornerstone of every credit application. Lack of confidence on the prospective borrower leads to a rejection of the proposal ab-initio.

The basis of this confidence is generally derived from the **5 'C's** of the prospective borrower i.e**. character, capacity, capital, collateral** and **conditions**. In addition to the 5 C's reliability, responsibility and resources are also looked into for gaining the confidence.

5.2.1.1.1. Character

Character is the paramount quality the lending Institution demands, while processing the Credit Proposal. The foundation of long term relationship with the Borrower commences with the favourable opinion formed by the Lender on the Character, Ability and Willingness of the Borrower, apart from looking into other aspects of "Background Check" or credit scoring.

The character of the borrower, which indicates his intention to repay, is very important even in contradicting situations, where the Borrower may have the ability to repay or totally be unable to repay. Willingness on his/ her part will somehow ensure complete repayment of the Loan. A questionable integrity would make every banker shun him/ her, even if backed by sufficient collaterals.

Character of a borrower is constituted by honesty, sobriety, good habits, personality, the ability and willingness to keep his word at all times and the honouring of the commitments under all circumstances.
Currently, there are means of knowing such integrity with the Central Bank of the country publishing list of defaulter's database.

Character of the borrower can also be gauged by an interaction with him/ her. The process of interaction also discloses the genuineness of purpose in his/ her mind.

5.2.1.1.2. Capacity:

The Capacity of the borrower reveals his/ her ability to stand in good stead in hours of crisis both financially and psychologically.

It deals with the ability of the borrower to manage an enterprise or venture successfully with the resources available to him. His/ the management team's educational, technical and professional qualifications, antecedents/ past track record of the enterprise, present activity, experience in the line of business, experiences of the family, special skill or knowledge possessed by him/ the collective knowledge base of the enterprise, his past record etc., would give an insight into his capacity to manage the show successfully and repay the loan.

5.2.1.1.3. Capital:

It is the amount to be brought in by the Borrower to stake his claim in the business i.e., borrower's margin. The owned funds concept being his/ her ability to meet the loss, if any, sustained in the Business and not solely depending on the Creditor/ Banker for the bail-out. This is also a minimum level of commitment anticipated from the Borrower by the Credit Appraisal Authorities.

However in respect of Venture Capital Funds, Innovative Ideas of the Borrowers take precedence over the Capital Infusion Arrangements.

5.2.1.1.4. Collateral:

Collateral means the type of security to be brought in by the Borrower, either in the form of tangible or intangible for securing the loan. Tangible refers to assets in physical form, while, intangible pertains to non–physical attributes such as, reputation, brand image, Goodwill, Patents and Trademark etc. Even a third party surety/ guarantee can be treated as intangible. The Collaterals are being stipulated depending upon the background of the borrower and also the quantum of finance sought by.
The collateral comes handy to the lenders to enforce the securities, in case of default committed by the borrowers. In case of tight monetary conditions prevailing in the market, higher collaterals are stipulated by way of margin on the quantum of finance being availed by the Borrowers.

5.2.1.1.5. Conditions:

The terms/ conditions stipulated by the credit lending authorities for availing loans are called as 'conditions'. It may be of pre-sanction/ post-sanction in nature.

Pre-sanction formalities relate to, adherence to certain terms and conditions and completion of documentation prior to disbursal of the loan Installments/ loan amount. Post-sanction formalities relate to compliance with the terms and conditions of the loan post disbursal.

For instance pre sanction formalities of compliance with certain conditions from the statutory authorities like the Tax/ the Municipal Authorities regarding fulfilling of the statutory obligations.

The post–sanction formalities confine mainly to the upkeep of collateral in good condition satisfying the requirement of the lending authorities.

Besides this, the following qualities of a borrower also help the bank in appraising the borrower for a lending decision – Competence, Initiative, Intelligence, Drive & Energy, Self-confidence, Frankness and Patience.

The 5Cs mentioned above are qualitative in nature and very difficult to compare with others. The below table is a suggestive nature to quantify the 5Cs of the prospective borrower. However, it is an only an indicative one, which can be used as a reference and is not a standard. The concept of Credit Scoring takes care of all these into account. In countries where Credit Scoring is not yet fully in vogue, due to various reasons like non-availability of unique Social security number, etc., this can be of use.

Table 2 – Quantification of 5Cs

#	Particulars	Excellent – 3 marks	Good – 2 marks	Poor – 1 mark
1.	Character	Honest. Keeps his words at all times.	Makes efforts to keep his words.	
2.	Personal Attention of Promoter	Fully involved and is the only source of income for the borrower.	Have other sources of income.	
3.	Competence	Has knowledge and experience in the line of activity and is assisted by able functionaries in key positions.	Has knowledge and experience in the line of activity and is assisted by professionals competent in the line of activity.	Has neither knowledge nor experience in the line of activity.
4.	Drive & Energy	From the front and fully involved.	Fairly energetic. Generally gets involved in all activities.	Avoid work.

#	Particulars	Excellent – 3 marks	Good – 2 marks	Poor – 1 mark
5.	Transparency	Speaks out about the weaknesses in the line of activity as well as the relative weakness of his business vis-à-vis the competitors.	Prepared to speak out about the weaknesses in the line of activity as well as the relative weakness of his business vis-à-vis the competitors, but after probing.	
6.	Confidence	Has complete self-belief.	Believes in his abilities.	
7.	Financial Resources	Proves his financial ability to not only meet the margin requirements, but also has buffer to finance over runs, delays etc.	Have resources to fund the margin as well as meet overruns marginally.	

The borrower appraisal is one of the challenging tasks in the appraisal process. In case of individual borrowers, background check and interview with the borrower may be sufficient. In the case of corporates, interview with each of the partners or directors and CxOs will be required. All the more such interview should be separately done and not together. Such an interviewing technique is unique and definitely is an art. Even before the entire appraisal methods were started to be used, banks were lending to different borrowers. The officials used to talk to the borrower for some time and decide whether to sanction loan to him or not. This is what is called as Borrower Interview and now aided with various methods, tools, reports, etc.

5.2.2. Technical Appraisal

The technical appraisal of a credit proposal involves a detailed study of the following aspects:

- Availability of basic infrastructure
- Selection of technology
- Availability of suitable technical process, raw material, skilled labour, etc.
- Licensing/ registration requirements

5.2.3. Management Appraisal

Management Appraisal also called as Management Evaluation by some schools is an important factor for a corporate customer. This will enable the bank to get satisfied about the managerial capability of the firm in managing the activities, generating funds and repaying the loans. Some vital areas of management appraisal:

- Actions of management of a company can have a bearing on the credit quality of a company and it is therefore very critical for credit analysts to evaluate the risks associated with the management of a company.
- Management evaluation primarily focuses on the goals and philosophies of the management which determine the business and financial risk of an entity.
- In evaluating a management, the past track record of the management in terms of its strategies, risk appetite, integrity and competence also needs to be examined in detail.
- Unlike other risks which credit analysts examine such as, Industry Risk, Business Risk and Financial risk, evaluating and assigning ratings to a management is always difficult as the parameters that are used to evaluate management are qualitative and subjective in nature.
- It is only through the experience of interacting with the management of many companies would an analyst be able to bring about a fine gradation between one management and the other.
- In case of large corporates information would be available with the rating agencies.
- Also the stock price, underlying reasons for movements of stock price, if it is a quoted company would give an idea about the management.

The other sources from where the banks do get information about the borrowers are:

- Newspaper reports.
- Public notices in newspapers etc.
- Scrutiny of balance-sheet and profit & loss accounts
- Websites

5.2.4. Financial Appraisal

This is the stage where all the financial statements, ratios, etc., are needed, to assess the solvency and repayment capacity of the firm. These were discussed in the earlier chapter in details. At this juncture, one important point to note is that the financial statements used for determining the quantum of loan required are all projected ones. Hence they would not be audited statements. There are instances that audited financial statements themselves being a fabricated one. If so, how about a projected financial statements. More so, there are various agencies to tailor make financial statements for the purpose of obtaining loans. Some of the warning signals for the banks while scrutinising the financial statements are listed below. These are cautioning areas where Banks cannot take it lightly. At the same time it is not always necessary that these areas may lead to non-performing or bad loans. It is only a caution from the experience.

- Steep decline in production figures
- Rising level of inventories, which may include large proportion of slow or non-moving items
- Larger and longer outstanding in bill accounts
- Longer period of credit allowed on sale documents negotiated through the bank and frequent return by the customers of the same as also allowing large discount on sales
- Failure to pay statutory liabilities
- Utilisation of funds for purposes other than running the units
- Delay in submission of financials, renewal data, etc.
- Showing reluctance to allow unit visits & abruptly reducing visits to bank branch
- Exclusion of some items of costs normally chargeable to manufacturing account
- By taking previous year's sales into current year
- Accounting sales made in the current year but deliverable in the next year

- Frequent change in accounting policies
- Deferring expenses
- Income smoothing – profits understatement
- Early recognition of revenues
- Under or over accrual of expenses
- Change in discretionary cost – manipulation of profits
- Low quality controls
- Frequent change of auditors
- Cash – restricted/ huge
- Receivables – large overdues, exposure to 1 or 2 clients only, slow turnover, frequent returns, related parties
- Inventories – large increase with no sales, slow turnover, faddish vs. jit, inadequate insurance, change in valuation methods, improper costing
- Investments – switching between current and non-current, overpricing, valuation methods, risky items should have been written off
- Fixed assets – change in depreciation policies, showing old and obsolete items, inadequate depreciation, high maintenance and repair costs, declining productivity, large written off assets
- Intangible assets – slow amortisation, huge goodwill vs. weak profit, high ratios of TNW
- Large and unreasonable dividends
- Declining profitability, sales volume
- Sudden Increase in debts
- Transfer of funds to sister concerns, etc.
- Rapid management turnover or poor quality of top management
- Bogus debtors
- Bogus investments
- Circular transactions among the group companies
- Write offs directly from reserves
- Investment – wrong/ reclassification
- Changes in methods of accounting
- Adjustments of losses against reserves
- Term debt – excess interest paid

In the same manner the financial statements can be manipulated by one or more ways – especially the projected ones:

- Inflate sales
- Reduce Expenses
- Defer Expenses

- Provide less than the required statutory amount to be provided
- Fiddle with other income
- Change the accounting method – contractor operations, depreciation, lease, etc.
- Actual Liability to Contingent Liability
- Fake Transactions

5.2.5. Market Appraisal

The purpose of the Market appraisal is to decide whether

- Demand projections made is reasonable based on:
  - Available survey
  - Industry Association projection
  - Independent market survey
- Whether marketing infrastructure is adequate like:
  - Distributing network
  - Transport facilities
  - Warehousing and stock level
- Competency of marketing personnel

5.2.6. Economic Appraisal

Economic appraisal is a type of decision method applied to a project that takes into account a wide range of costs and benefits, denominated in monetary terms or for which a monetary equivalent can be estimated. Economic Appraisal is a key tool for achieving value for money and satisfying requirements for decision accountability. It is a systematic process for examining alternative uses of resources, focusing on assessment of needs, objectives, options, costs, benefits, risks, funding, affordability and other factors relevant to decisions.
The main types of economic appraisal are:

- Cost-benefit analysis
- Cost-effectiveness analysis
- Scoring and weighting

Economic appraisal is a methodology designed to assist in defining problems and finding solutions that offer the best value for money (VFM). This is especially important in relation to public expenditure and is often used as a vehicle for planning and approval of public investment relating to policies, programmes and projects.

The principles of appraisal are applicable to all decisions, even those concerned with small expenditures. However, the scope of appraisal can also be very wide. Good economic appraisal leads to better decisions and VFM. It facilitates good project management and project evaluation. Appraisal is an essential part of good financial management, and it is vital to decision-making and accountability.

5.2.7. Environmental Appraisal

Environmental appraisal needs to be assessed in case of projects that might have any adverse effects on the environment. Have remedial measures been included in the project design? How will the project impact on quality of and likely damage & the cost of restoration - Air, Water, Noise, Vegetation, Human life, etc.

Major projects, such as these, cause environmental damage

- Power plants
- Irrigation schemes
- Industries like bulk drugs, chemicals and leather processing.

5.3. Assessment of working capital:

The working capital requirements of a firm shall be assessed by adopting any of the following five methods, depending on the type of the business activity/ categories of borrowers as per the bank's lending policy. These methods are primarily followed by banks in India. However, with some minor differences, almost same methods are followed in other countries also.

- Turnover Method recommended by Nayak Committee
- First Method of Lending
- Second Method of Lending
- Cash Budget System

The quantum of Bank finance will normally be restricted to the amount of funds locked up less a certain percentage as margin. The margins stipulated will depend on various factors like salability of materials, whether imported or indigenous, quality, durability, price fluctuations in the market for the commodity etc.

Further to the various guidelines issued and after giving weightage to the various factors that flow into the fixing of the policy, the Banks need to decide on the policy for the various types of borrowers.

The success of an Organisation, among other things, is largely dependent on the person behind the Venture. Every credit proposal therefore, small or big, is backed by an entrepreneur who apart from investing Capital will also have to invest substantial amount of time.

Every project which may be considered technically feasible, economically viable and financially sound may run into difficulties if it is not properly managed by a competent person who understands the risk and is willing to take, manage and knows how to mitigate them.

5.3.1. Different Committees – Indian System

After first phase of nationalisation of banks in 1969, the banking system in India was in the stabilisation mode. In 70s it was passing through a liquidity crunch. Hence the regulators wanted to restrict free flow credit and limitations were fixed for working capital finance. In this connection various committees were formed and they gave different recommendations.

A study group headed by Shri Prakash Tandon, the then Chairman of Punjab National Bank, was constituted by the RBI in July 1974 with eminent personalities drawn from leading banks, financial institutions and a wide cross-section of the industry with a view to study the entire gamut of Bank's finance for working capital and suggest ways for optimum utilisation of Bank credit. This was the first elaborate attempt by the central bank to organise the Bank credit. Most banks in India even today continue to look at the needs of the corporates in the light of methodology recommended by the Group. The report of this group is widely known as Tandon Committee report.

The weaknesses in the Cash Credit system have persisted with the non-implementation of one of the crucial recommendations of the Committee.

In the background of credit expansion seen in 1977-79 and its ill effects on the economy, RBI appointed a working group to study and suggest:

- Modifications in the Cash Credit system to make it amenable to better management of funds by the Bankers and ii) alternate type of credit facilities to ensure better credit discipline and co relation between credit and production. The Group was headed by Sh. K.B. Chore of RBI and was named Chore Committee.
- Another group headed by Sh. P.R. Nayak (Nayak Committee) was entrusted the job of looking into the difficulties faced by Small Scale Industries due to the sophisticated nature of Tandon & Chore Committee recommendations. His report is applicable to units with credit requirements of less than ₹50 lakhs.
- The recommendations made by Tandon Committee and reinforced by Chore Committee were implemented in all Banks and Bank Credit became much more organised. However, the recommendations were perceived as too strict by the industry and there has been a continuous clamor from the Industry for movement from mandatory control to a voluntary market related restraint. With recent liberalisation of economy and reforms in the financial sector, RBI has given the freedom to the Banks to work out their own norms for inventory and the earlier norms are now to be taken as guidelines and not a mandate. In fact, beginning with the slack season credit policy of 1997-98, RBI has also given full freedom to all the Banks to devise their own method of assessing the short term credit requirements of their clients and grant lines of credit accordingly. Most banks, however, continue to be guided by the principles enunciated in Tandon Committee report.

5.3.2. Turnover Method

This method of working capital loan appraisal, recommended by Nayak Committee, is applicable for small loans say upto ₹ 1 crore. The appraisal method is very simple.

- The maximum working capital limit should be 20% of projected annual turnover.
- The unit should be required to bring in 5% of their annual turnover as margin money.
- In other words, 25% of the output or annual turnover value should be computed as the quantum of working capital required out of which 20% can be financed by the bank and remaining met by the own funds.

- Nayak committee guidelines were framed assuming an average production/ processing cycle of 3 months (i.e. WC would be turned over 4 times in a year).
- If the operating cycle is less than three months and the working capital requirement is less than 20% of the turnover, banks will discuss with the borrower and the consent would be obtained.
- If the operating cycle is more than three months, there is no restriction on extending finance at more than 20% of the turnover provided that the borrower should bring in proportionally higher stake in relation to his requirement of bank finance.

An example:

Details	₹ in 000's
Projected turnover	1,200 (A)
Working capital requirement @25% of (A)	300 (B)
Let the liquid surplus be assumed as	20 (C)
Less: Liquid surplus or 5% of (A) whichever is higher	60 (D)
Maximum Permissible Bank Finance (B - D)	240

Some important points for appraisal in this method:

- It is to be ensured that the projected annual turnover is reasonable and achievable by the unit and further, the estimated growth if any over the previous year is realistic.
- The concerned staff at branch may find that the returns filed with statutory authorities as useful guiding documents for verification of sales and assessment of reasonableness of the projections.
- The entire sale proceeds should be routed through the Cash Credit account of the unit.
- Date of actual sales pertaining to the last five years, estimated for the current year, and projected for the next year, together with the trend analysis of the relative industry, would also be useful while appraising the sales projections.
- Other information regarding modernisation, expansion of the existing manufacturing capacity, government policies, taxation and other relevant internal and external factors also need to be taken into account.
- Any projection say beyond 15% of the previous year actual or current year estimates would need closer look.

5.3.3. First Method of Lending

The Tandon committee norms had laid out the methodology for inventory and receivable norms, while, the Chore Committee prescribed methods of lending for large WC limits.

This was in a regime of credit shortages and it held sway for over two decades. However with the wave of de-regulation sweeping the banking industry, it was not long before freedom was given to the Banks to evolve their own norms for assessment of limits. Various banks have used this freedom to evolve their own methodology for assessment of limits but most have still revolved around the second of lending as postulated by the Tandon committees.

This still is being widely used, as the methodology considers all the sources of funds the borrower can access and arrives at the finance the bank would extend. Cash credit system has given way to loan system for assessing working capital, both short and medium term. To meet the short term working capital demands, Working Capital Demand Loan is sanctioned. On the other hand the medium term loans are for boosting Net working capital.

There is the Working Capital Demand Loan for short term while the medium term loans are for boosting Net working capital at times.
First Method of Lending – an example:

Figures in ₹ in lakhs

Current Assets (CA)	200
Current Liabilities	40
Working Capital Gap	160
Less Margin - 25% of WCG (Min NWC)	40
Maximum Permissible Bank Finance	120
Current Liabilities including bank finance (CL)	160
Current Ratio (CA/CL)	1.25

5.3.4. Second Method of Lending

There is not much of difference between the first and second methods of lending excepting in calculating the margin:

Second Method of Lending – an example:

Figures in ₹ in lakhs

Current Assets (CA)	200
Current Liabilities	40
Working Capital Gap	160
Less Margin - 25% of CA	50
Maximum Permissible Bank Finance	110
Current Liabilities including bank finance (CL)	150
Current Ratio (CA/CL)	1.33

The first and second methods have become the guiding factors for assessment. The final approved limits may be within this cap. At times this may also be called the projected balance sheet method as limits are approved on the basis of next year's realistic projected performance.

In case of consortium and multiple banking system, after assessing the overall requirement the bank may fix its limits based on allotted share or the share it wants to take up in the case of multiple banking arrangements. This share becomes the cap for the limit.

5.3.5. Third Method of Lending

In addition to the first and second method of lending, there was one other called Third method – this method recommended a concept called Working Capital Term Loan. As per this method a fixed amount of cash credit loan should be treated as Term Loan and repayed periodically.

There was not much welcome both by borrowers and by the banks for this method and hence this did not kick off well.

5.3.6. Cash Budget System

This method of appraisal is suitable for service industries or non-manufacturing industries. This is also applicable for seasonal industries wherein the working capital requirement is not uniform across the year. Agriculture, Cash Crops, Fertilizer, Commodities, Construction/ Infrastructure projects, etc., are some of the industries falling under this category.

In this method a cash budget is made out for the season or the entire year, keeping in view the procurement needs, payments for production expenses and receipts. The limits are assessed keeping in view the peak cash deficit. The monitoring is done based on the Cash Budgets as approved by the sanctioning committee.

5.4. Quantum and Margin

The quantum of Bank finance will be normally restricted to the amount of funds locked up less a certain percentage of margin. The margins stipulated will depend on various factors like salability, whether imported or indigenous, quality, durability, price fluctuations in the market for the commodity etc. The cardinal rule of credit is NEED BASED and shall not exceed the actual requirement of the borrower in each case.

At the same time if banks do not lend adequately, it is equivalent to killing the unit.

Hence all the above methods provide the calculation for maximum permissible bank finance (MPBF).

5.4.1. CMA Data

For periodical review of the functioning of the unit and availment of the facilities sanctioned, banks do collect various data called CMA Data.

In the system of working capital assessment the required data are generally collected from the borrowers in the following formats.

- Form I - Particulars of existing/ proposed limits form the banking system
- Form II - Operating statement
- Form III - Analysis of balance sheet
- Form IV - Comparative Statement of CA/ CL
- Form V - Computation of MPBF working capital
- Form VI - Funds flow statement

Information provided in the Forms II, III, IV and VI serve the detailed financial analysis. The Form V which is used for computation of MPBF. In Form I information relating to working capital and term loan borrowings (existing and proposed) is obtained. Additional information regarding borrowings from term lending institutions for WC purposes and lease finance availed will also be collected in form I. From the data presented in a published balance sheet of a borrower, their CA and CL are now analysed as per the classification given in Form III. The classification is done to arrive at the current ratio and net working capital of the borrower to evaluate their liquidity. But some of the items of CA/ CL are excluded for computation of MPBF.

Projected levels of inventory and receivables are now examined in the assessment exercise in relation to the trend of past levels, and inter firm comparison of the levels. The levels are then normally accepted if they are within the indicative norms advised by the RBI. In the case of creditors, past trend and inter firm comparison serve as the basis for the verification.

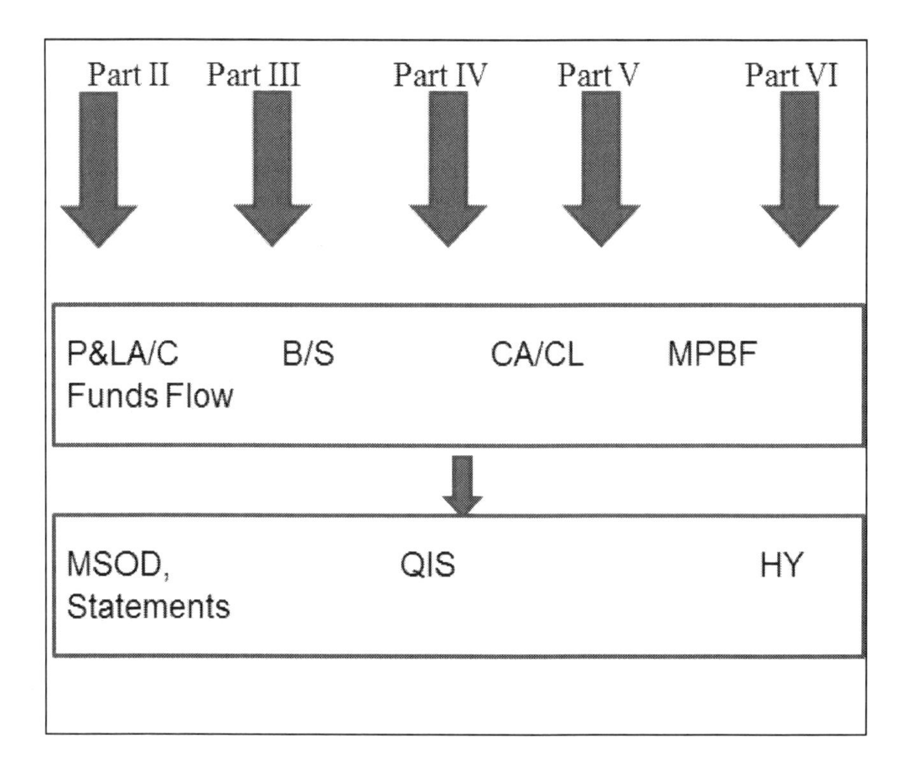

Figure 4 – CMA Linkage

5.5. Chapter Summary

What is Credit Appraisal? – To assess the capacity and inclination of the borrower and to ensure end use.

The credit appraisal process involves multiple steps to arrive at the final decision. It is imperative that the scope for errors/ omissions is minimised/ eliminated. The controls operating in the bank business environment have to be dynamic in order to be effective.

First and foremost is the Bank's Credit Policy in tune with the policy of Government and/ or Central Bank of the country.

In general anyone is tempted to conclude the credit appraisal is appraising through financial statements. Though this is an important area in the credit appraisal, there are various other appraisals that influence the lending decision viz., Borrower Appraisal, Technical Appraisal, Management Appraisal, Market Appraisal, Economic Appraisal and Environmental Appraisal.

There are various Cautions and Warning signs noted in this book itself and something more which are not explicitly mentioned. These are to be carefully noted so that the loan is sanctioned to the mutual benefit of the borrower and the bank.

Two base rules of credit are – Need Based lending and Adequate lending. It is better not to lend than under lending. This will kill the business – it cannot be closed neither it cannot be run. To do the appraisal in a scientific method, the systems, reports and various parameters can help the bank. However the technique of Borrower appraisal and interviewing him is an art, which can be prudently done only by an experienced banker.

*****

Chapter 6. Trade Finance

What is trade finance? There are various definitions to be found as to what trade finance is and the choice of words used is interesting. It is described both as a 'science' and as "an imprecise term covering a number of different activities". As is the nature of these things, both are accurate. In one form it is quite a precise science managing the capital required for international trade to flow. Yet within this science there are a wide range of tools at the financiers' disposal, all of which determine how cash, credit, investments and other assets can be utilised for trade.

In its simplest form, a seller requires a buyer to prepay for goods shipped. The buyer naturally wants to reduce risk by asking the exporter to document that the goods have been shipped. The buyer's bank assists by providing a letter of credit to the seller (or the seller's bank) providing for payment upon presentation of certain documents, such as a bill of lading, etc. The seller's bank may make a loan to the seller on the basis of the sale and purchase contract.

For those borrowers enjoying fund based working capital limits of say ₹ 500 lakhs or more from the banking system, it shall be ensured to finance a minimum of 25% of the credit sales by way of bills. It shall also be ensured that the limits sanctioned against book debts shall not exceed 75% of the aggregate limits sanctioned to the borrower for financing his credit sales. Bills discounting limits may be sanctioned to the constituents after a proper appraisal of their credit needs.

6.1. Stakeholders in Trade Finance

Various players are involved in any Trade Finance activity. Some of the main players with their roles and the documents are listed in this table. The documents are discussed later in this chapter:

Table 3 – Players in Trade Finance

Player	Role	Documents handled
Seller, also called as exporter in the case of international trade	Sale of goods	Brochure for the products, Invoice, Packing list, Declarations to customs/

Player	Role	Documents handled
		Central Bank of the country Transport Documents, Certificate of origin
Buyer also called as importer in the case of international trade	Buying the goods	Confirmed Order Letter of Credit application
Buyer's Bank	Issuance of LC, Intimation of LC through correspondent bank	LC application Reimbursement agreement with the buyer
Seller's Bank	Negotiation of bills under LC, Sending Bills for collection	Letter of Credit
NOSTRO/ VOSTRO maintaining Bank	The bank with whom the importer/ exporter maintain accounts	Funds transfer – acting on SWIFT messages
SWIFT system	Message communication	Various funds messages
Transporters	Transporting the goods	Shipper – Bill of Lading Airways – Air way Bill Lorry transporter – Lorry Receipt Railways – Railway receipt
Forwarding Agents	Arranges for transporting of goods	Freight Forwarders receipt
Insurance Companies	Insuring the goods	Insurance policy – Marine, Air, Road.
Custom Authorities	Enforcing the import/ export trade regulations	SDF – Self declaration forms GR forms
Central Bank of the country	Monitors Inflow/ outflow of foreign exchange	Checking of export/ imports with GR forms/ statement submitted by

Player	Role	Documents handled
		Foreign Exchange Authorized Dealers
Shipping and Clearing agents for both buyer and seller	Booking/ clearing of goods	
Chambers of Commerce		Certificate of Origin
Advisory agencies like credit rating		Rating of sovereign, banks, importers/ exporters, etc.
Market Research Organisations		Research report about the market, etc.

6.2. Trade financing

Trade finance aims at reducing transaction cost and time by streamlining trade procedures and processes. One of the most important challenges for traders involved in a transaction is to secure financing so that the transaction may actually take place. The faster and easier the process of financing an international transaction, the more trade will be facilitated. The major purpose of Trade Finance would be:

- Traders require working capital (i.e. short-term financing) to support their trading activities.
- Exporters will usually require financing to process or manufacture products for the export market before receiving payment. Such financing is known as pre-shipment finance.
- Conversely, importers will need a line of credit to buy goods overseas and sell them in the domestic market before paying for imports. In most cases, foreign buyers expect to pay only when goods arrive, or later still if possible, but certainly not in advance. They prefer an open account, or at least a delayed payment arrangement. Being able to offer attractive payments term to buyers is often crucial in getting a contract and requires access to financing for exporters.

6.3. Trade Financing Products

The main types of trade financing instruments/ products are as follows and the major among them are explained in detail:

- Inland Trade Finance
- International Trade Finance
- Bills backed by LC
- Clean Bills
- Hundi based trade
- Bills of Exchange – Payable
    - On Demand
    - At sight
    - Usance Bills
- Supply Bills – Bills drawn on Government Departments & Corporate.

6.3.1. Documentary Credit

This is the most common form of the commercial letter of credit. The issuing bank will make payment, either immediately or at a prescribed date, upon the presentation of stipulated documents. These documents will include shipping and insurance documents, and commercial invoices. The documentary credit arrangement offers an internationally used method of attaining a commercially acceptable undertaking, by providing for payment to be made against presentation of documentation representing the goods, making possible the transfer of title to those goods. A letter of credit is a precise document whereby the importer's bank extends credit to the importer and assumes responsibility in paying the exporter. A common problem faced in emerging economies is that many banks have inadequate capital and foreign exchange, making their ability to back the documentary credits questionable. Exporters may require guarantees from their own local banks as an additional source of security, but this may generate significant additional costs as the banks may be reluctant to assume the risks. Allowing internationally reputable banks to operate in the country and offer documentary credit is one way to effectively solve this problem.

6.3.2. Pre-Shipping Financing

This is financing for the period prior to the shipment of goods, to support pre-export activities like wages and overhead costs. It is especially needed when inputs for production must be imported. It also provides additional working capital for the exporter. Pre-shipment financing is especially important to smaller enterprises because the international sales cycle is usually longer than the domestic sales cycle. Pre-shipment financing can take in the form of short-term loans, overdrafts and cash credits.

6.3.3. Post-Shipment Finance

This is financing for the period after the shipment of goods. The ability to be competitive often depends on the trader's credit term offered to buyers. Post-shipment financing ensures adequate liquidity until the purchaser receives the products and the exporter receives payment. Post-shipment financing is usually short-term.

6.3.4. Buyer's Credit

A financial arrangement whereby a financial institution in the exporting country extends a loan directly or indirectly to a foreign buyer to finance the purchase of goods and services from the exporting country. This arrangement enables the buyer to make payments due to the supplier under the contract.

6.3.5. Supplier's Credit

A financing arrangement under which an exporter extends credit to the buyer in the importing country to finance the buyer's purchases.

6.3.6. Trust Receipt

An importer can get a loan from a bank based on the LC and the goods LC promises that he will be getting. Funds can be borrowed against the future sale of those goods.

6.3.7. Packing Credit

With an LC, the exporter can get an overdraft or loan for a particular shipment of goods. It can be in the form of pre-shipment financing –

repayment is made when goods are shipped or post-shipment finance – repayment is made when the buyer has paid for the goods.

6.3.8. Short Term Finance

A trader might need financing on a short-term basis. For instance, sellers might need to offset the purchase of goods by paying them. They can get external financing in a number of ways.

6.3.9. Overdraft

An overdraft (or line of credit) offered by banks is the most common method for obtaining funds quickly and easily. Traders overdraw their current account up to a maximum amount agreed with the bank. Interest is paid only on what is overdrawn.

6.3.10. Revolving Credit Agreement

Traders can arrange with a bank to have an agreed amount of funds made available to them. They can withdraw and top up the funds regularly. For this, they pay the bank a fee in a lump sum or a percentage of the average unused balance.

6.3.11. Term Loan

If a trader can provide some form of collateral, such as a property, he/ she can apply for a bank loan. Before granting the loan, the bank will consider factors such as its relationship with the trader, the trader's credit history, the purpose, amount and duration of the loan, and the trader's cash flow to repay the loan.

6.3.12. Transaction Loan

When traders receive a firm order for their goods, they can approach the bank for a transaction loan to buy materials and pay for expenses for that particular order. The more well-known and credible the customer placing the order, the more favorable banks will be in granting the loan.

6.3.13. Inventory Financing

Traders with unsold stock can approach finance companies to provide them funds using the inventory as collateral. This is given on a revolving basis so as to encourage traders to make inventory sales to repay funds. Sometimes the finance companies require the trader to agree to a factoring arrangement before granting the loan.

6.3.14. Factoring

This involves the sale at a discount of accounts receivable or other debt assets on a daily, weekly or monthly basis in exchange for immediate cash. The debt assets are sold by the exporter at a discount to a factoring house, which will assume all commercial and political risks of the account receivable. In the absence of private sector players, governments can facilitate the establishment of a state-owned factor or a joint venture set-up with several banks and trading enterprises.

Exporters can make use of factoring companies to get cash. A factoring company takes the unpaid invoices of goods and collects on behalf of the exporter. This way, the exporter gets paid upfront and does not need to wait for the goods to be delivered or take the risk that the customer may not pay.

6.4. Documents relating to Trade Finance

Uniform Customs and Practice for Documentary Credits (UCPDC) is the general reference used to have a uniform interpretation of trade finance jargons across the globe. This explains the various documents used in trade finance industry.

Different documents used in Trade Finance Industry are:

- Quotation/ Proforma Invoice
- Samples
- Order
- Commercial Invoices
- Delivery Challan
- Packing List
- Certificate

- LC – Inland/ Foreign
- Insurance Documents
- Certificate of origin
- Statutory requirements: Customs Clearance , GR Forms
- Proof of Dispatch of Goods:
    - Airway Bill
    - Ocean Bill of Lading,
    - Road, Rail or Inland Waterway Transport Documents
    - Courier and Post Receipts
    - Transport Documents Issued by Freight Forwarders
    - Freight Forwarders Receipt, Combined Transport Document

Most of the above documents are self-explanatory. However, some of the major documents are explained below:

6.4.1. Letter of Credit (LC)

Before exporting a particular shipment of goods, the exporter asks for a Letter of Credit (LC). This is a letter of undertaking/ guarantee from the buyer's bank to pay an exporter, through the exporter's bank, for goods on behalf of the buyer. This gives the exporter the assurance that goods will be paid on delivery. It also means the importer does not need to pay for the goods before they have been delivered. An LC is used as a convenient means of payment in international trade and opens up other financial facilities also.

6.4.2. Transport Documents

Depending on the mode of transport, the transport document differs. However, its role is same. Some of the transport documents are:

6.4.2.1. Bill of Lading

The transport document or bill of lading is a pivotal document in the letter of credit transaction. It serves at least 3 functions:

- It is evidence of a contract of carriage between the shipper and the carrier, giving the terms and conditions of carriage.
- It is the shipper's receipt for the goods delivered to the carrier

- It is a document of title to the goods. The possessor of the original bill of lading is the only one with the right to reclaim the goods from the carrier.

6.4.2.2. Air Waybill

The air waybill or air consignment note serves the same function for air transport as the bill of lading does for marine and rail transport. It is evidence given by the carrier that the goods have been received by him.

6.4.2.3. Freight Forwarder's Receipt

A freight forwarder is a firm or individual that arranges for the shipment of goods for others for a fee, and is often referred to as a forwarding agent or forwarder. The receipt issued by him is known as Freight Forwarder's Receipt.

6.4.3. Export Credit Insurance

In addition to financing issues, traders are also subject to risks, which can be either commercial or political. Commercial risk arises from factors like the non-acceptance of goods by buyer, the failure of buyer to pay debt, and the failure of foreign banks to honor documentary credits. Political risk arises from factors like war, riots and civil commotion, blockage of foreign exchange transfers and currency devaluation. Export credit insurance involves insuring exporters against such risks. It is commonly used in Europe, and increasing in importance in the United States as well as in developing markets. The types of export credit insurance used vary from country to country and depend on traders' perceived needs. The most commonly used are as follows:

- Short-term Export Credit Insurance – Covers periods not more than 180 days. Protection includes pre-shipment and post-shipment risks, the former covering the Period between the awarding of contract until shipment. Protection can also be covered against commercial and political risks.
- Medium and Long-term Export Credit Insurance – Issued for credits extending Longer periods, medium-term (up to three years) or longer. Protection provided for financing exports of capital goods and services.
- Investment Insurance – Insurance offered to exporters investing in foreign countries.

- Exchange Rate Insurance – Covers losses as a result of fluctuations in exchange rates between exporters' and importers' national currencies over a period of time.

6.5. Business Process

General Trade Finance Business process would be:

6.5.1. Pre-Contractual Phase

- Buyer identifies products or services and possible sources of supply
- Seller offers the range of products to the targeted buyer/s
- Buyer responds to the offer with a request to send quotation and samples.

6.5.2. Contractual Phase

- Buyer issues a confirmed order
- Seller accepts the order
- A formal relationship between buyer and seller, covering contract negotiation and validation operations.
- Contract Creation covering the payment terms
- Contract Management - compliance against contract/ Contract Validation)

6.5.3. Logistics Phase

- Packing and Labeling
- Delivery of Goods (Shipment)
- Logistics
- Work in Progress status
- Buyer request his Banker to issue Letter of Credit (LC) in favour of seller for payment guarantee
- Buyer's Bank issue LC as per the terms of the order
- Buyer's Bank intimating the LC through correspondent bank known as advising bank and confirming bank in case the bank confirms the LC
- Seller's Bank provides pre-shipment finance (working capital) to seller for procurement & production.
- Seller Informs Buyer about the readiness of the goods for shipment.

- Seller gets certification from Inspection agencies as per LC requirement.
- Seller makes arrangement for freight through logistic agencies-transport/ shipping/ railway/ airway companies, forwarding agents.
- Seller raises Invoice on getting confirmation from buyer
- Seller insures the goods through Insurance companies.
- Seller applies for necessary clearance from custom authorities.
- Seller furnish the details of transaction to Central Bank of the Country

6.5.4. Settlement Phase

- Seller exports the goods through his shipping and clearing agent
- Seller submits the packing list along with documents required under LC being proof of shipment to Seller's Bank.
- Invoicing
- Payment authorisation
- Payment scheduling, Payment status tracking
- Seller's Bank negotiates/ purchases/ collects the bills under LC and provides credit for the goods shipped.
- Seller's Bank sends the bills to Buyer's Bank with payment request to credit his NOSTRO account.
- Buyer's Bank checks the documents submitted for compliance with the terms of the contract.
- On complying of terms, pays the Bank account
- Claim reimbursement from Buyer as per the agreement.
- Buyer receives the goods through his shipping and clearing agent.
- Inspection of goods by the buyer
- Buyer pays the amount to his Bank.
- On receipt of credit, seller's bank adjusts the credit, if any extended and credit the proceeds to seller account.
- Discounts/ rebates
- Receipts of Goods
- Validation of Invoices to PO receipts
- Cancellation/ Rejection of Order
- Claims/ Dispute Management/ Discrepancy Approval/ Chargeback Management
- Charges on late payment and Discounts on early payment

6.5.5. Post-Processing Phase

- MIS reports, trade statistics, analytics
- Stakeholder performance history (also risk details) based on the past performance (Scorecard)

6.6. Chapter Summary

Bill finance is an important type of working capital finance to help both the sellers and buyers in helping to rotate funds. Some of the forms of trade finance can include Documentary collection, trade credit insurance, export factoring and forfaiting. Some forms are specifically designed to supplement traditional financing, such as "transactional equity", which can assist the borrower in funding the down payment required by a bank before it extends credit.

Trade Finance has been reviewing the global trade market since 1983. The remit of what is covered somewhat broad, and as the market evolves to meet the requirements of financing global trade, hence content has changed.

Opening of Letters of Credit (LCs) and purchase/ discount/ negotiation of bills under LCs would normally be done only in respect of genuine commercial and trade transactions of a borrowable constituents who have been sanctioned regular credit facilities by a bank. Fund based facilities (including bills financing) or non-fund based facilities like opening of LCs, providing guarantees and acceptances would not be extended to non-constituent borrowers of the bank or as a non-constituent member of a consortium/ multiple banking arrangement.

For the purpose of credit exposure, bills purchased/ discounted/ negotiated under LCs or otherwise shall also be reckoned on the borrower constituent. Such exposure will attract a risk weightage of 100% for capital adequacy purposes (as is applied for funded limits).

In trade finance a caution about the below Warning signals have to be noted by the banks:

- Bogus / Fake Bills
- Customer –transport Operator tie up
- Over invoicing

- Description of Goods different
- Accommodation Bills
- Discounting of Bill with Bank and taking cash from buyer direct
- Not advising the bank about return of goods
- In collusion with Bank Officials committing fraud.
- Group co bills, service bills
- Round figures

*****

Chapter 7. Non-Fund Based Lending

The credit facilities given by the banks where actual bank funds are not immediately involved are termed as "non-fund based facilities". These facilities are divided in three broad categories as under:

- Letters of credit
- Guarantees
- Co-acceptance of bills/ deferred payment guarantees

For a corporate customer, a percentage of working capital facility is always sanctioned as non-fund based limits. The collaterals provided for the funded facilities are also extended to these facilities.

Units for the above facilities are also simultaneously sanctioned by banks while sanctioning other fund based credit limits.

Facilities for co-acceptance of bills/ deferred payment guarantees are generally required for acquiring plant and machinery and may, technically be taken as a substitute for term loan which would require detailed appraisal of the borrower's needs and financial position in the same manner as in case of any other term loan proposal.

7.1. Letters of Credit

Bank would normally open letters of credit for their own customers who enjoy credit facilities with them. Customers maintaining current account only and not enjoying any credit limits should not be granted LC facilities except in cases where no other credit facility is needed by the customer.

Letter of credit is a method of settlement of payment of a trade transaction and is widely used to finance purchase of machinery and raw material etc. It contains a written undertaking given by the bank on behalf of the purchaser to the seller to make payment of a stated amount on presentation of stipulated documents and fulfilment of all the terms and conditions incorporated therein. All letters of credit in India relating to the foreign trade i.e., export and import letters of credit are subject to provisions of 'Uniform Customs & Practice for Documentary Credits' (UCPDC). These provisions neither have the status of law or automatic application but parties to a letter of credit bind themselves to these provisions by specifically agreeing to do so. These provisions have almost universal application and help to arrive at unambiguous interpretation of various terms used in letters of credit and also set the obligations, responsibilities and rights of various parties to a letter of credit.

Inland letters of credit may also be issued subject to the provisions of UCPDC and it is, therefore, important that customers should be fully aware of these provisions and shall also understand complete LC mechanism as these transactions will find increasing use in the coming days. Complete text of UCPDC is not being reproduced. However, important articles have been given as extracts wherever necessary. An attempt has been made to explain the LC mechanism in full as there are some inherent risks and wrong notions while dealing with these transactions.

7.1.1. Definition of a Letter of Credit

Article 2 of UCPDC defines a letter of credit as - The expressions "documentary credit(s) and standby letter(s) of credit" used herein (hereinafter referred to as 'credit(s)' means any arrangement, however, named or described whereby a bank (the issuing bank), acting at the request and on the instructions of a customer (the applicant of the credit) or on its own behalf:

i. Is to make a payment to or to the order of a third party (the "beneficiary"), or is to accept and pay bills of exchange (Draft(s)) drawn by the beneficiary, or
ii. Authorises another bank to effect such payment, or to accept and pay such bills of exchange (Draft(s)), or
iii. Authorises another bank to negotiate against stipulated document(s), provided that the terms and conditions of the credit are complied with.

For the above purposes even the branches of the same bank in different countries are considered another bank.

Letter of credit is a written undertaking by a bank (issuing bank) given to the seller (beneficiary) at the request and in accordance with the instructions of buyer (applicant) to effect payment of a stated amount within a prescribed time limit and against stipulated documents provided all the terms and conditions of the credit are complied with".

Letters of credit thus offers both parties to a trade transaction a degree of security. The seller can look forward to the issuing bank for payment instead of relying on the ability and willingness of the buyer to pay. He is further assured of payment being received on due date enabling him to have proper financial planning. The only condition being attached is submission of stipulated documents and compliance with the terms and conditions of credit. The buyer on the other hand will be obliged to pay only after receipt of documents of title to goods to his satisfaction.

Letter of credit is an independent document in itself as provided vide article 3 of UCPDC which states that: "Credits, by their nature, are separate transactions from the sales or other contract(s) on which they may be based and banks are in no way concerned with or bound by such contract(s), even if any reference whatsoever to such contract(s) is included in the credit." This article is very important and has a direct bearing on the relationship of the opener with bank. Many disputes have arisen due to the reference of sale contract in the letter of credit. The letter of credit is issued in accordance with the instructions of the applicant who should provide complete and precise instructions to the bank to avoid any dispute later. The undertaking of a bank to pay, accept and pay drafts or negotiate and/or to fulfil any other obligations under the credit is not subject to claims or defences by the Applicant resulting from his relationship with the issuing Bank or the Beneficiary.

Another very important provision which is very vital to letter of credit operations is regarding disputes emanating from the quality/quantity of goods covered under a letter of credit. Article 4 of UCPDC states:

"In credit operations all parties concerned deal with documents, and not with cods, services and/ or other performances to which the documents may relate.

An important point which emerges from the above article is that any dispute regarding the quality/ quantity of the goods may have to be settled outside the terms of letter of credit. Letter of credit thus provides no protection on this account and the applicant must specify submission of necessary weight certificate/quality analysis certificates etc. as considered necessary to satisfy himself regarding the goods on the basis of these documents alone.

7.1.2. Parties to a Letter of Credit

There are various parties to a Letter of Credit. Some of these players are already mentioned in the earlier chapter. However for completeness they are repeated here:

Table 4 – Parties in an LC

#	Party	Role
1.	Applicant/ Opener	It is generally the buyer of the goods who gets the letter of credit issued by his banker in favour of the seller. The person on whose behalf and under whose instructions the letter of credit is issued is known as applicant/ opener of the credit.
2.	Opening bank/ issuing bank	The bank issuing the letter of credit
3.	Beneficiary	The seller of goods in whose favour the letter of credit is issued
4.	Advising Bank	Notification regarding issuing of letter of credit may be directly sent to the beneficiary by the opening bank. It is, however, customary to advise the letter of credit through some other bank operating at the place/ country of seller. The bank which advises the letter of credit to the beneficiary is known as advising bank.
5.	Confirming Bank	A letter of credit substitutes the credit worthiness of the buyer with that of the issuing bank. It may sometimes happen especially in import trade that the issuing bank itself is not widely known in the exporter's country and exporter is not prepared to rely on the LC opened by that bank. In such cases the opening bank may request other bank usually in the country of exporter to add its confirmation which amounts to an additional undertaking being given by that bank to the beneficiary. The bank adding its confirmation is known as confirming bank. The confirming bank has the same liabilities towards the beneficiary as that of opening bank.

#	Party	Role
6.	Negotiating Bank	The bank that negotiates the documents drawn under letter of credit and makes payment to beneficiary.

P.S. The function of advising bank, confirming bank and negotiating bank may be undertaken by a single bank only.

7.1.3. Letter of Credit Mechanism

Any business/ industrial venture will involve purchase transactions relating to machine/other capital goods and raw material etc., and also sale transactions relating to its products. The customer may, therefore, find himself on either side of a LC transaction at different times depending upon his position at that particular moment. He may be an applicant for a letter of credit for his purchases while be the beneficiary under other letter of credit for his sale transaction. It is, therefore, necessary that complete LC mechanism covering the liabilities and rights of both the applicant and the beneficiary are understood for maximum advantage.

The complete mechanism of a letter of credit may be divided in three parts as under:

Issuing of Credit: Letter of credit is always issued by the buyer's bank (issuing bank) at the request and on behalf and in accordance with the instructions of the applicant. The letter of credit may either be advised directly or through some other bank. The advising bank is responsible for transmission of credit and verifying the authenticity of signature of issuing bank and is under no commitment to pay the seller.

The advising bank may also be required to add confirmation and in that case will assume all the liabilities of issuing bank in relation to the beneficiary as stated already. The below diagram describes the complete process of issuance of credit.

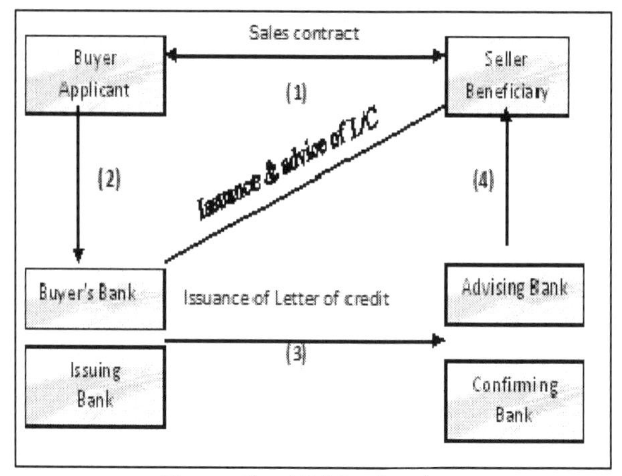

Figure 5 – LC Mechanism

Negotiation of Documents by beneficiary - On receipt of letter of credit, the beneficiary shall arrange to supply the goods as per the terms of LC and draw necessary documents as required under LC. The documents will then be presented to the negotiating bank for payment/acceptance as the case may be. The negotiating bank will make the payment to the beneficiary and obtain reimbursement from the opening bank in terms of credit.

Settlement of Bills Drawn under Letter of Credit by the opener - The last step involved in letter of credit mechanism is retirement of documents received under LC by the opener. On receipt of documents drawn under LC, the opening bank is required to closely examine the documents to ensure compliance of the terms and conditions of credit and present the same to the opener for his scrutiny. The opener should then make payment to the opening bank and take delivery of documents so that delivery of goods can be obtained by him.

7.1.4. Types of Letters of Credit

The 'Letters of Credit' may be divided in two broad categories as under:

- **Revocable letter of credit.** This may be amended or cancelled without prior warning or notification to the beneficiary. Such letter of credit will not offer any protection and should not be accepted as beneficiary of credit.
- **Irrevocable letter of credit.** This cannot be amended or cancelled without the agreement of all parties thereto. This type of letter of

credit is mainly in use and offers complete protection to the seller against subsequent development against his interest.

It may, however, be mentioned here that every letter of credit must clearly indicate whether it is revocable or irrevocable. In the absence of such indication the credit shall be deemed to be irrevocable. The beneficiary, on receipt of credit, must therefore, examine that the letter of credit is not indicated as revocable.

The letter of credit may provide drawing of documents either on D.P. basis in which case the documents will be delivered against payment or on D.A. basis in which case the documents will be delivered against acceptance. The letter of credit may also call either for demand documents which are required to be paid on presentation or usance documents, the payment of which will be required to be made after an agreed period of usance. All these will be required to be settled at the time of finalising the sale contract and clear instructions to the bank in this regard will have to be given at the time of opening of the letter of credit.

There are a few special types of credits in vogue offering a degree of convenience in operations. Brief details of these credits are given below:

Revolving Letter of Credit: The concept of revolving letter of credit is best illustrated by the following example:

Let us presume that goods of the total value of ₹ 60 lakhs are required to be purchased over a period of one year and requirement of those goods at a time is proximately ₹ 10 lakhs. If the terms of payment are under LC the buyer may have two options as under:

- To open an LC for ₹ 60 lakhs valid for 1 year and permit part shipment, or
- To open letters of credit for ₹ 10 lakhs each on six different occasions.

Option (i) not only requires very high limits from the bank but will result in high cost of operations by way of commission charges. Option (ii) involves a lot inconvenience as the LC will be required to be opened six times.

To obviate such difficulties, a revolving LC can be opened under which the amount of LC is renewed/ reinstated after the original LC amount has been utilised. Thus a revolving LC for ₹ 10 lakhs valid for one year may be opened in the above case. After negotiation and settlement of bills drawn under this LC, the LC amount may again be reinstated by the bank. The amount reinstated in such a manner will again become available for negotiation.

Transferable Letter of Credit: A transferable letter of credit is one that is transferred by the original (first) beneficiary to one or more second beneficiaries. It is normally used when the first beneficiary does not supply the merchandise himself but is a middleman and thus wishes to transfer part or all of his rights and obligations to actual suppliers as second beneficiaries.

The letter of credit is transferable only if it is specifically stated as transferable. In case the credit is silent about it, the LC will be deemed to be transferable. Further the LC can be transferred only once which in other words means that second beneficiary cannot transfer it to any other person. Under a transferable letter of credit the second beneficiary assumes the same rights and obligations as that of the original beneficiary.

The transfer of credit is, however, not to be confused with the right of assignment of benefits to which the beneficiary may become entitled under a letter of credit. The beneficiary is having right to assign the proceeds to which he may become entitled under the provisions of applicable law even in case of non-transferable credits.

These transferable credits are very much in vogue in export trade. The important points to be noted while dealing with transferable credits are stated below:

The LC should clearly indicate that it is transferable. In the absence of such indication the LC would be deemed to be not transferable. The first beneficiary under a transferable LC has a right to transfer in part or whole to other parties (second beneficiaries). For this purpose he has to request the advising bank to issue an advice of transfer to the second beneficiary(ies). The charges of the bank for effecting transfer are payable by the first beneficiary unless otherwise stated.

The advice of transfer issued by the bank along with copy of the original credit will be taken as a complete letter of credit for almost all practical purposes.

Back to Back letter of Credit. A letter of credit which is backed by other letter of credit is termed as 'back to back' credit and is also used when middleman is involved in a sale transaction. Such transaction offers additional security of the letter of credit to the bank issuing back to back LC. However, for successful completion of the entire transaction it must be ensured that back to back LC is opened on the worse terms as compared to the terms under; the original letter of credit.

Red Clause Letter of Credit: All letters of credit as discussed above provide a sort of guarantee of payment against documents which are drawn strictly in terms of subject letter of credit. In other words the benefit of LC accrues only when shipment of goods is completed. Red Clause Letter of Credit goes a step further and authorises the advising bank to grant an advance to the beneficiary at the pre-shipment stage itself. The advance by the advising bank shall be recovered at the time of negotiation of documents under that LC. In case, however, no shipment is effected by the beneficiary and he fails to present documents under LC, the bank making advance under red-clause letter of credit will claim reimbursement of advance made from the issuing bank.

7.1.5. Precautions

Important points/ precautions which must be noted by the openers/ beneficiaries at various stages of operations under a letter of credit are now discussed hereunder:

7.1.5.1. At the Time of Opening of a Letter of Credit

- Letter of credit offers almost complete protection to the seller but the buyer is put to many disadvantages and has to make payments against documents only. Before agreeing to open a letter of credit in favour of the seller, the opener must be satisfied with the creditworthiness and general reputation of the seller. Entire success of an LC transaction depends on proper conduct of the seller. Confidential report on the seller must be obtained at the time of first transaction with him.
- Letter of credit also does not offer any protection for the quality/ quantity of goods supplied under the LC. It would, therefore, be necessary to know the nature of goods and specify submission of quality reports/ inspection reports from an independent agency to ensure receipt of goods of proper quality This is particularly important in case of import of chemicals and such other goods.
- The opener has to submit an LC application to the opening bank. The instructions contained in the LC application are the mandate for the

issuing bank and letter of credit will be issued in accordance with this application. It is, therefore, necessary that complete and precise information must be given in the LC application form specifying therein the description, unit rate and quantity of the goods covered under IX and details of documents required in absolute clear and unambiguous terms. The reference to underlying sale contract must be avoided as far as possible. The LC application must nevertheless contain all the required/ information based on which LC could be opened by the bank.

- After the LC has been issued by the bank, a copy thereof must be obtained immediately. The LC must be scrutinised to ensure that it has been properly issued and is in conformity with LC application. Discrepancy, if any, must be brought to the notice of opening bank immediately.

7.1.5.2. At the time of Receipt and Negotiation of LC

- On receipt of LC from the opening/ advising bank, the beneficiary must ensure that the letter of credit is advised without any superimposed clause. Sometimes an unauthenticated message may be received and advised by the bank which may not be acted upon unless authenticity of the message (LC) is confirmed by the advising bank.
- The LC must state on the face of it that it is irrevocable and must have been issued by a bank of repute. If the issuing bank is not widely known, confirmation from a local bank may be insisted upon before acting on such a Credit.
- The LC must be scrutinised to ensure that the terms indicated are in conformity with the underlying sale contract. It does not contain any ambiguous clauses and documents required therein can be completed. If it has some conditions which cannot be complied with, the matter should immediately be taken up with opener for amendment of LC. Shipment of goods before ensuring that all the terms and conditions can be complied with may be risky as no protection will be offered under LC.
- Necessary arrangement for shipment/despatch of goods shall be made after acceptance of LC. The shipment and despatch must be made as per the terms of LC and well within the period prescribed under LC.
- After shipment of goods necessary documents must be prepared. Extreme care must be taken to prepare the documents as the payment will be dependent upon the acceptance of those documents under the LC. Even a minor mistake in spelling or punctuation may prove to be enough ground for rejecting the documents. It is necessary that

complete knowledge of all the Articles of UCPDC relating to documents must be obtained at the time of preparation of documents.

- The documents, complete in all respects, should then be presented to the bank for negotiation. The negotiating bank must be requested to closely examine the documents and indicate the discrepancies, if any. Efforts should then be made to remove those discrepancies and documents free of all discrepancies only must be negotiated.
- There may sometimes be some discrepancies which cannot be rectified and two options are now available as under:
  - (a) Get confirmation/ authority of opening bank to negotiate discrepant documents, or
  - (b) Get the documents negotiated under reserve after giving suitable indemnity bond to the negotiating bank.
- The option (a) is more advantageous as it will ensure final payment at the time of negotiation itself. The option (b) may be exercised only in exceptional circumstances as 'negotiation under reserve' does not offer any guarantee as to acceptance of documents under LC.
- The final authority of acceptance of documents lies with the opening bank only, who has to be given reasonable time for scrutinising the documents. Documents under LC are negotiated by banks in India with recourse and if the documents are subsequently rejected by opening bank due to any reasons the negotiating bank will recover the amount from the beneficiary. It is, therefore, necessary that documents are always drawn strictly in conformity with the terms of LC.

On receipt of advice of rejection of documents the negotiating bank must be instructed to initiate necessary steps to safeguard the interest of the beneficiary in light of various provisions of UCPDC.

7.1.5.3. On Receipt of Documents under LC

The negotiating bank will transmit the documents to the opening bank after negotiation and obtain reimbursement in terms of the LC. The opening bank will be given a reasonable time to scrutinise the documents and decide whether the documents are drawn in accordance with the terms of credit and are acceptable or to reject the documents. Reasonable time has since been specified by Article 13(b) of UCPDC and it is not to exceed seven banking days following the day of receipt of the documents. In case documents are rejected by the opening bank, it must give due notice of such rejection to the negotiating bank by fastest means and also place the documents at the disposal of the negotiating bank. The receipt of documents will also be advised by the opening bank to the applicant.

- Applicant must independently scrutinise the documents received under LC and ensure that the documents can be accepted. In case any discrepancy is noted in the documents which are not acceptable, the documents must be rejected and an immediate notice should be given to the opening bank for such rejection. The opening bank may be instructed to take up the matter with negotiating bank suitably. Notice of rejection must invariably be given to the opening bank in writing.
- The documents if acceptable, must be taken upon due date for which necessary financial arrangement shall be made in advance.

7.2. Guarantees

A contract of guarantee can be defined as a contract to perform the promise, or discharge the liability of a third person in case of his default. The contract of guarantee has three principal parties as under:

i. Principal debtor - the person who has to perform or discharge the liability and for whose default the guarantee is given.
ii. Principal creditor - the person to whom the guarantee is given for due fulfilment of contract by principal debtor. Principal creditor is also sometimes referred to as beneficiary.
iii. Guarantor or Surety - the person who gives the guarantee.

Banks provides guarantee facilities to its customers who may require these facilities for various purposes. The guarantees may broadly be divided in two categories as under :

i. **Financial guarantees** – Guarantees to discharge financial obligations to the customers. Financial guarantees will be issued by the banks only if they are satisfied that the customer will be in a position to reimburse the bank in case the guarantee is invoked and the bank is required to make the payment in terms of guarantee.
ii. **Performance guarantees** – Guarantees for due performance of a contract by customers. Performance guarantee will be issued by the banks only on behalf of those customers with whom the bank has sufficient experience and is satisfied that the customer has the necessary experience and means to perform the obligations under the contract and is not likely to commit any default.

The conditions relating to obligant being a customer of the bank enjoying credit facilities as discussed in case of letters of credit are equally applicable for guarantees also. In fact, guarantee facilities also cannot be sanctioned in isolation.

As a rule, banks will guarantee shorter maturities and leave longer maturities to be guaranteed by other institutions. Accordingly, no bank guarantee will normally have a maturity of more than 10 years.

Banks should not normally issue guarantees on behalf of those customers who enjoy credit facilities with other banks.

As a rule, banks should avoid giving unsecured guarantees in large amounts and for medium and long term period. They should avoid undue concentration of such unsecured guarantee commitments to particular groups of customer and/ or trades.

Unsecured guarantees on account of any individual constituent should be limited to a reasonable proportion of the bank's total unsecured guarantees. Guarantees on behalf of individual should also bear a reasonable proportion to constituent's equity.

In exceptional cases, banks may give deferred payment guarantees on an unsecured basis for modest amounts to first class customers who have entered into deferred payment arrangements in consonance with Government policy. But such unsecured guarantees should be accommodated within the limits indicated above.

Guarantees executed on behalf of any individual constituent, or a group of constituents, should be subject to prescribed exposure norms.

When any bank reaches a stage where it is likely to exceed the norm, it should not undertake any further commitment on account of guarantees.

Suitable arrangements may be made to keep a watch from time to time about the outstanding guarantees of the bank so as to ensure that it does not exceed the norm.
It is essential to realise that guarantees contain inherent risks and that it would not be in the bank's interest or in the public interest generally to

encourage parties to over-extend their commitments and embark upon enterprises solely relying on the easy availability of guarantee facilities.

The guarantees are issued by the banks against counter guarantees given to the banks by the customer. The banks may also require a cash margin and/ or other securities as per sanction.

7.3. Co-acceptance of Bills

Acceptance of a bill: Process by which a buyer (called a 'drawee') accepts the seller's bill of exchange by signing under the words 'accepted' on face of the bill. By this act, the drawee becomes the acceptor and converts the bill into a post-dated cheque, an unconditional obligation to pay it on or before its maturity date. Since the seller may not know about the genuineness of the buyer, he may insist on the buyer's bank to co-accept the bill. It is another version of LC or guarantee.

Limits for co-acceptance of bills will be sanctioned by the banks after detailed appraisal of customer's requirement is completed and the bank is fully satisfied about the genuineness of the need of the customer. Further customers who enjoy other limits with the bank should be extended such limits.

Only genuine trade bills shall be co-accepted and the banks should ensure that the goods covered by bills co-accepted are actually received in the stock accounts of the borrowers. The valuation of goods as mentioned in the accompanying invoice should be verified to see that there is no overvaluation of stocks.

The banks shall not extend their co-acceptance to house bills/ accommodation bills drawn by group concerns on one another.

Where banks open LC and also co-accept bills drawn under such LC, the discounting banks, before discounting such co-accepted bills, must ascertain the reason for co-acceptance of bills and satisfy themselves about the genuineness of the transaction.

Co-acceptance facilities will normally not be sanctioned to customers enjoying credit limit with other banks.

7.4. Chapter Summary

The Modern Banking Functions are Fund based and Non-Fund based. These functions of a bank are those in which banks extend various services to their customers or add their commitments to certain transactions undertaken by their clients and charge their fees/ commissions for the services rendered by them/ their commitments added to the transactions undertaken by the clients. These activities are popularly known as "Non-fund based facilities" provided by Banks. The major non-fund based facilities that are considered as a part of regular credit facilities are:

- Letter of Credit
- Bank Guarantees and
- Co-acceptance of bills.

As a part of their Non-fund based functions banks allow Letter of Credit and Bank Guarantee facilities for their customers to meet their requirements. These are facilities allowed to the customers by the banks. But there is no outflow of funds from the banks immediately. However, at any point of time, in future, banks may have to shell out money and hence they are called "Contingent Liabilities" in the balance sheet of the banks.

*****

Chapter 8. Credit and Borrower Rating

There are three related areas about rating for lending purposes – like:

- Credit Rating
- Credit Scoring
- Borrower Rating

8.1. Credit Rating

A **credit rating** evaluates the credit worthiness of an issuer of specific types of debt, specifically, debt issued by a business enterprise such as a corporation or a government. It is an evaluation made by a credit rating agency of the debt issuers' likelihood of default.

Credit ratings are determined by credit ratings agencies. The credit rating represents the credit rating agency's evaluation of qualitative and quantitative information for a company or government; including non-public information obtained by the credit rating agencies/ analysts.

Credit ratings are not based on mathematical formulae. Instead, credit rating agencies use their judgment and experience in determining what public and private information should be considered in giving a rating to a particular company or government. For instance, the credit rating of a bond, is used by individuals and entities that purchase the bonds issued by companies and governments to determine the likelihood that the government will pay its bond obligations.

A poor credit rating indicates a credit rating agency's opinion that the company or government has a high risk of defaulting, based on the agency's analysis of the entity's history and analysis of long term economic prospects.

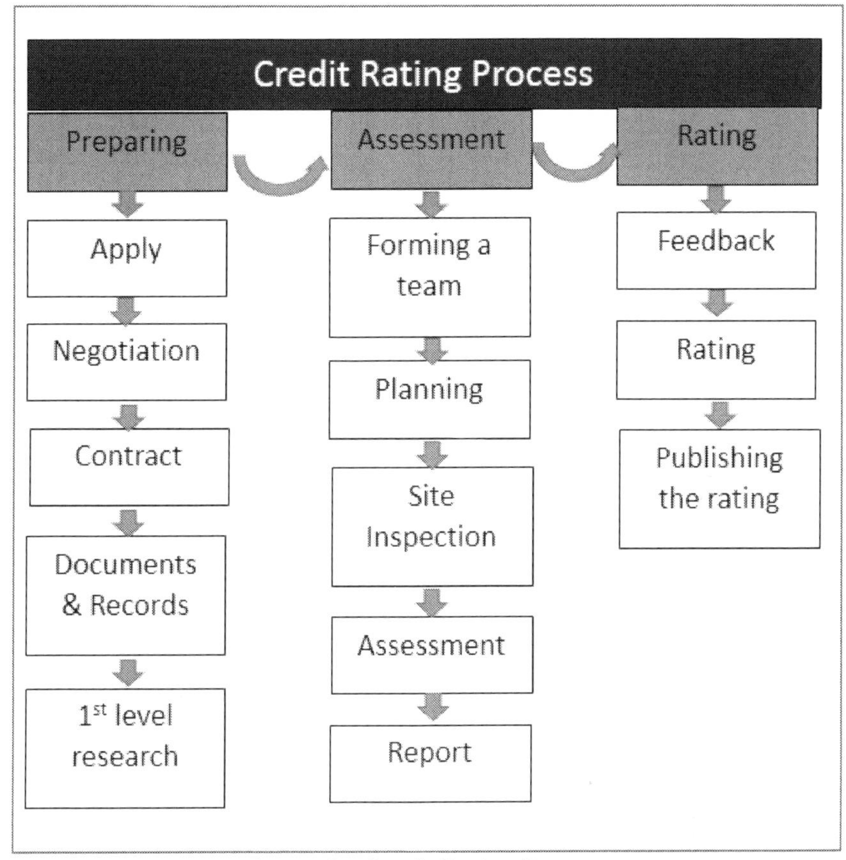

Figure 6 – Credit Rating Process

8.1.1. Sovereign Credit Ratings

A **sovereign credit rating** is the credit rating of a sovereign entity, i.e., a national government. The sovereign credit rating indicates the risk level of the investing environment of a country and is used by investors looking to invest abroad. It takes political risk into account. Ratings are further broken down into components including political risk, economic risk. Euro money's bi-annual country risk index monitors the political and economic stability of 185 sovereign countries.

8.1.1.1. Short-term rating

A short-term rating is a probability factor of an individual going into default within a year. This is in contrast to long-term rating which is evaluated over a long timeframe. In the past institutional investors preferred to consider long-term ratings. Nowadays, short-term ratings are commonly used.

First, the Basel agreements require banks to report their one-year probability if they applied internal-ratings-based approach for capital requirements. Second, many institutional investors can easily manage their credit/bond portfolios with derivatives on monthly or quarterly basis. Therefore, some rating agencies simply report short-term ratings.

8.1.2. Corporate credit ratings

The credit rating of a corporation is a financial indicator to potential investors of debt securities such as bonds. Credit rating is usually of a financial instrument such as a bond, rather than the whole corporation. These are assigned by credit rating agencies such as A. M. Best, Dun & Bradstreet, Standard & Poor's, Moody's or Fitch Ratings and have letter designations such as A, B, C.

Some of the major global credit rating agencies are: Dun & Bradstreet, Moody's, Standard & Poor's and Fitch Ratings. Other agencies include A. M. Best (U.S.), Baycorp Advantage (Australia), Egan-Jones Rating Company (U.S.), Global Credit Ratings Co. (South Africa), Japan Credit Rating Agency, Ltd. (Japan), Muros Ratings (Russia alternative rating agency), and Rapid Ratings International (U.S.). CRISIL, Fitch, ICRA and CARE are the major credit rating agencies in India.

The Standard & Poor's rating scale is as follows, from excellent to poor: AAA, AA+, AA, AA-, A+, A, A-, BBB+, BBB, BBB-, BB+, BB, BB-, B+, B, B-, CCC+, CCC, CCC-, CC, C, D. Anything lower than a BBB- rating is considered a speculative or junk bond.

The Moody's rating system is similar in concept but the naming is a little different. It is as follows, from excellent to poor: AAA, Aa1, Aa2, Aa3, A1, A2, A3, Baa1, Baa2, Baa3, Ba1, Ba2, Ba3, B1, B2, B3, Caa1, Caa2, Caa3, Ca, and C.

A. M. Best rates from excellent to poor in the following manner: A++, A+, A, A-, B++, B+, B, B-, C++, C+, C, C-, D, E, F, and S.

The CTRISKS rating system is as follows: CT3A, CT2A, CT1A, CT3B, CT2B, CT1B, CT3C, CT2C and CT1C. All these CTRISKS grades are mapped to one-year probability of default.

Table 5 – Comparison Credit Ratings

Moody's		**S&P**		**Fitch**		
Long-term	Short-term	Long-term	Short-term	Long-term	Short-term	
Aaa	P-1	AAA	A-1+	AAA	F1+	Prime
Aa1		AA+		AA+		High grade
Aa2		AA		AA		
Aa3		AA-		AA-		
A1		A+	A-1	A+	F1	Upper medium grade
A2		A		A		
A3	P-2	A-	A-2	A-	F2	
Baa1		BBB+		BBB+		Lower medium grade
Baa2	P-3	BBB	A-3	BBB	F3	
Baa3		BBB-		BBB-		
Ba1	Not prime	BB+	B	BB+	B	Non-investment grade speculative
Ba2		BB		BB		
Ba3		BB-		BB-		
B1		B+		B+		Highly speculative
B2		B		B		
B3		B-		B-		
Caa1		CCC+	C	CCC	C	Substantial risks
Caa2		CCC				Extremely speculative
Caa3		CCC-				In default with little
Ca		CC				
		C				

Moody's		S&P		Fitch		
						prospect for recovery
C		D	/	DDD	/	In default
/				DD		
/				D		

The major criteria based on which the Rating Agencies decide the credit ratings are:

- Objectivity - the rigor of the analytical techniques used
- Independence - ensuring the institution is free from political and economic pressure
- Transparency - the public availability of the rating methodologies and broad availability of assessments
- Disclosure - the disclosure of technical model factors such as the definition of default, and the time horizon of assessments
- Resources - the availability of expertise and information to ensure assessments are carried out correctly
- Credibility - from an internal perspective the criteria for assessing credit grades, and from an external perspective, widespread acceptance and use of the grades

8.2. Credit Score

A **credit score** is a numerical expression based on a statistical analysis of a person's credit files, to represent the creditworthiness of that person. A credit score is primarily based on credit report information typically sourced from credit bureaus.

Lenders, such as banks and credit card companies, use credit scores to evaluate the potential risk posed by lending money to consumers and to mitigate losses due to bad debt. Lenders use credit scores to determine who qualifies for a loan, at what interest rate, and what credit limits. Lenders also use credit scores to determine which customers are likely to bring in the most revenue. The use of credit or identity scoring prior to authorizing access or granting credit is an implementation of a trusted system.

Credit scoring is not limited to banks. Other organisations, such as mobile phone companies, insurance companies, landlords, and government departments employ the same techniques. Credit scoring also has a lot of overlap with data mining, which uses many similar techniques. This technique is not prevalent in India. There is an initiative for Credit Score currently being evaluated by the Government and an agency crisil which can be developed in future.

Regardless of whether the appraisal process is manual or mechanized, in the retail front, most banks use a framework by name "Credit Scoring" to evaluate individual proposals. Under this, marks are assigned to various parameters/ attributes that find a place in the proposal. And using varying weights for different parameters, an aggregate score, otherwise called "Credit Score" is arrived at for individual borrowers/ proposals. And if the Credit Score is more than the minimum threshold acceptable to the bank, the proposal is sanctioned. Conversely, if the Credit Score for a particular borrower is less than the minimum threshold, then the proposal stands rejected.

8.2.1. Building Credit Scoring Models

In simple terms, Credit Scoring is a statistical model that reckons the rules and laws of statistics for evaluating individual borrowers. While using a credit scoring model could be easier, designing it is not. For building a credit scoring model, first one has to identify the various factors that need to be reckoned in the model. Obviously, these factors should be relevant to the performance of individual loan accounts. Hence, any bank building a model takes a look at the performance of its past retail credit accounts. From them, using a tool such as factor analysis or discriminate analysis, it identifies those parameters that seem to have an influence on account performance. Having identified the various parameters, it needs to assign correct weights for each such parameter. This again is better done by using the historical data. Once this is done, the credit scoring model built **is** validated through back-testing. If the model passes such a validation exercise, then it is accepted for usage.

8.2.2. Using Credit Scoring Models

Once a credit scoring model is accepted for use, it is for the bank to ensure that all its credit proposals necessarily have information on those parameters reckoned by the model. For instance, if the credit scoring model reckons the location of the borrower's postal address as a parameter for credit decision, then the proposal form needs to have address information of the prospective borrower. (Incidentally, some of the banks brand certain areas as "negative zip codes" in each city).

8.2.3. DMS vs. DSS

Having a credit scoring model in place makes retail credit decision that much easier. Nonetheless, when banks use automated credit scoring, they may end up in the horns of a dilemma whether to use the same as a decision making system (DMS) or decision support system (DSS). If it were to be a DMS, effectively there would be no decision making role at all for the retail credit manager. He/ she becomes a mere spectator to the entire process of credit sanction or rejection. On the other hand, if the automated appraisal system were to be just a DSS, then all credit decisions have to be finally taken by the credit manager, which may negate the very purpose of automation. One way to resolve this DMS -DSS dilemma could be to keep the system DMS *vis-à-vis* those proposals that have very high or very low credit scores and let the system refer other proposals to the credit manager where the credit scores come in the grey area. In such limited and borderline cases, the individual retail credit manager may apply his/ her mind, exercise his/ her discretion and arrive at a final decision.

8.2.4. Credit Scoring — Static and Dynamic Models

Credit scoring models can be designed to be static or dynamic. In the case of a static model, the various parameters for which scores are to be assigned as well as the weights to be reckoned for each such parameter are pre-defined/ hard-coded. Hence, such a model cannot on its own modify the parameters or the weights. In other words, such a model would be too rigid to be of real use. On the contrary, dynamic credit scoring models need to be learning systems driven. Such a credit scoring model keeps assessing on an on-going basis the transactional behavior of various individual borrower accounts already sanctioned/ disbursed. On the basis of its observations, it checks whether the parameters currently being used are relevant and whether any new ones need to be used. Also the current weights are reviewed and modified when and where necessary. Such an automatic review and updation of the model can be designed to be carried out either periodically or on a real time basis. Given the system load, a periodic updation looks desirable. Nonetheless, individual banks may have different preferences in this regard.

8.2.5. In-House & Outsourced Models

Credit scoring models used by banks are of two types. Some banks develop in-house proprietary models and use them for credit appraisal/ decision. On the other hand, internationally, there are reputed agencies that provide credit scores of individual loan applicants on demand. In fact, in the US, credit scores are often outsourced by retail banks/ financial institutions from reputed agencies such as Equifax, Trans Union or Esperion. The advantage of an in-house proprietary model is that it lets the individual bank reckon all those factors it thinks that are relevant for credit decision. Such freedom may not be available if credit scores/ scoring models are outsourced. But the downside is developing proprietary models could be prohibitively expensive. Besides, agencies that offer credit scores on outsourcing basis also act as credit bureaus and maintain updated credit sensitive information on individuals.

In the Indian context, as far as the understanding goes, there are no industry standard credit scoring models available for outsourcing. Again, in India, only very recently a credit bureau with a focus on individual borrowers has come into existence. It could take some mote time for it to make a difference to the retail credit appraisal process being followed by individual banks.

8.2.6. Credit Scoring Models – Pros and cons

As it happens with most things, credit scoring models too have their pluses and minuses. In the first place, credit scoring models, especially the automated ones, can help banks handle huge volume of proposals. In fact, without credit scoring models, the cost of retail credit appraisal could get prohibitively expensive. Again, automated credit scoring can dramatically quicken the timeframe required for decision making. Given the fact that retail credit front is competitive, now banks are vying with each other in cutting down their "turnaround time" for individual credit proposals. Sticking on to such competitive and ever-shrinking deadlines would be more or less impossible without having an automated credit scoring methodology in place. Of course, the most important advantage of credit scoring models is that they make the appraisal process totally unbiased. Prospective borrowers are assessed on the basis of certain quantifiable parameters and credit decisions arrived at. On the other hand, in a manual appraisal model, two individual credit managers may sometime have different views *vis-à-vis* one particular proposal.

This should not mean that credit scoring models are panacea. They come with their own luggage of defects and demerits. First of all, every credit scoring model is just as good as its underlying algorithm. Obviously, it can't prove any better. Thus, if the basic algorithm of a credit scoring model were defective, the flaw would get transmitted to the entire credit decision making process. Another serious issue that could affect the efficacy of any credit scoring model is its inability to reckon the material impact of disclosures in credit proposals. Nor can they be in a position to check willful omission or commission of information. On this front, in fact, credit scoring models may as well miss the wood for the trees. Credit scoring models that are learning-system driven suffer from another defect too. They get easily misled by wanton and mass defaults. Any knee-jerk adjustment in parameters and weights affected by the model in response to such defaults could condition the future performance of the model. Besides, all learning system driven credit scoring models work on the premise that future is a replica of the past. This way they tend to over extend the past into the future. Such a premise may not always lead to correct appraisal or credit decisions.

8.2.7. Factors that Influence Credit Score

The major factors that influence the credit score are:

- Amount owing on accounts
- Amount owing on specific types of accounts
- Lack of a specific type of balance, in some cases
- Number of accounts with balances
- Proportion of credit lines used (proportion of balances to total credit limits on certain types of revolving accounts)
- Proportion of installment loan amounts still owing (proportion of balance to original loan amount on certain types of installment loans)

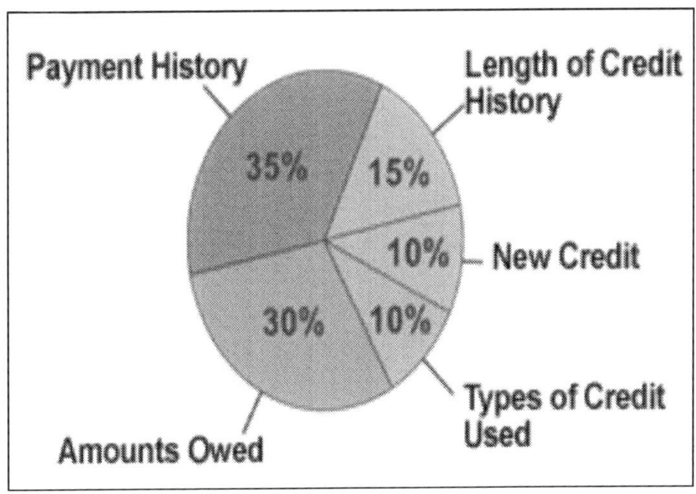

Figure 7 – Credit Score Parameters

8.2.8. Credit Scoring System - A Globetrot

Though the basic principles and application of Credit Scoring are same, the usage and systems may vary from region to region. Let us discuss some of them.

8.2.8.1. Australia

In Australia, credit scoring is widely accepted as the primary method of assessing credit worthiness. Credit scoring is not only used to determine whether credit should be approved to an applicant, but credit scoring is also used in the setting of credit limits on credit cards/store cards, in behavioral modeling such as collections scoring, and also in the pre-approval of additional credit to a company's existing client base.

Although logistic (or non-linear) probability modeling is still the most popular means by which to develop scorecards, various other methods offer extremely powerful alternatives, including MARS, CART, CHAID, and random forests. At present Veda Advantage, the main provider of credit file data only provides a negative credit reporting system which contains information on applications for credit and adverse listings indicating a default under a credit contract. This makes accurate credit scoring difficult for banks if they have no existing relationship with a prospective borrower.

8.2.8.2. Austria

In Austria credit scoring is done as a blacklist. Consumers which did not pay bills end up on the blacklists that are held by different credit bureaus. Having an entry on the black list may result in the denial of contracts. Just specific branches like telecom carriers use the list on a regular basis. Banks do not use these lists, but rather inquire about securities and income of the consumer when giving out loans. According to the Austrian Data Protection Act, consumers must opt-in for the use of their private data for any purpose. Consumers can also retrieve the permission to use the data later, which makes any further distribution or use of the collected data illegal. Consumers also have the right to get a free copy of all data held by the credit bureaus once a year. Wrong or unlawfully collected data must be deleted or corrected.

8.2.8.3. Canada

The system of credit reports and scores in Canada is very similar to that in the United States, with two of the same reporting agencies active in the country: Equifax and Transunion. There are, however, some key differences. One such difference is that, unlike the United States, where a consumer is allowed only one free copy of their credit report a year, in Canada, the consumer may order a free copy of their credit report any number of times in a year, as long as the request is made in writing, and as long as the consumer asks for a printed copy to be delivered by mail. This request by the consumer is noted in the credit report, but it has no effect on their credit score. Two of the leading credit scores are Equifax Credit Score, which range between 280 to 850 while FICO (Fair Isaac Corporation) credit score ranges between 300 and 850.

The Government of Canada offers a free publication called *Understanding Your Credit Report and Credit Score*. This publication provides sample credit report and credit score documents, with explanations of the notations and codes that are used. It also contains general information on how to build or improve credit history, and how to check for signs that identity theft has occurred. The publication is available online at the Financial Consumer Agency of Canada. Paper copies can also be ordered at no charge for residents of Canada.

8.2.8.4. India

The Credit Information Bureau (India) Limited (CIBIL) was incorporated in 2000 by the Government of India and the Reserve Bank of India to provide credit information about commercial and consumer borrowers to a limited group of members, including banks, financial institutions, non-banking financial companies, housing finance companies and credit card companies.

8.2.8.5. Norway

In Norway, credit scoring services are provided by three credit scoring agencies: Dun & Bradstreet, Experian and Leinsdorf Decision. Credit scoring is based on publicly available information such as demographic data, tax returns, taxable income and any *Betalingsanmerkning* (non-payment records) that might be registered on the credit scored individual. Upon being scored, an individual will get a notice (written or in the form of an e-mail) from the scoring agency stating who performed the credit score as well as any information provided in the score. In addition, many credit institutions use custom made scorecards based on any number of parameters. Credit scores range between 300 and 900.

8.2.8.6. South Africa

Credit scoring is used throughout the credit industry in South Africa, with the likes of banks, micro-lenders, clothing retailers, furniture retailers, specialised lenders and insurers all using credit scores. Currently two of the three main retail credit bureau offer credit bureau scores. Transunion (formerly ITC) offer the Empirical Score which is, as of mid-2010, in its 4th generation. The Empirical score is segmented into two suites: the account origination (AO) and account management (AM). Experian South Africa likewise have a Delphi credit score with their fourth generation about to be released (late 2010).

8.2.8.7. Sweden

Sweden also has a system for credit score. This system aims to find people with bad payment attitude. It has only two levels, good and bad. Anyone who does not pay a requested debt payment on time, and also not after a reminder, will have their case forwarded to the Swedish Enforcement Administration, a national authority which collects debts. The very appearance of a company as a debtor in this authority, will render a mark among private credit bureaus - however, this does not apply to a private person. This mark is called *Betalningsanmärkning* (non-payment record) and can according to the law be stored for three years for a private person and five years for a company. This kind of non-payment record will make it very difficult to get a loan, a rental apartment, a telephone subscription or a job with cash handling. The banks of course use income and asset figures in connection with loan assessments.

If one gets an injunction to pay by the Enforcement Administration, it is possible to object to it. Then the one requesting the payment must show the correctness in district court. Failure to object is seen as admitting the debt. If the debtor loses the court trial, costs for the trial are added to the debt. Taxes and authority fees must always be paid on request unless payment has already been made.

Every person with a Swedish national identification number must register a valid address, even if living abroad, since sent letters are considered to have arrived. For example, the Swedish astronaut Christer Fuglesang has a *Betalningsanmärkning* since he forgot to pay the Stockholm congestion tax, and had an old invalid address registered, since he lives in the US. Letters with payment requests did not reach him on time.

8.2.8.8. United Kingdom

The most popular statistical technique used in UK is logistic regression to predict a binary outcome, such as bad debt or no bad debt. Some banks also build regression models that predict the amount of bad debt a customer may incur. Typically, this is much harder to predict, and most banks focus only on the binary outcome.

Credit scoring is only closely regulated by the Financial Services Authority when used for the purposes of the Advanced approach to Capital Adequacy under Basel regulations. It is very difficult for a consumer to know in advance whether they have a high enough credit score to be accepted for credit with a particular lender. This is due to the complexity and structure of credit scoring, which differs from one lender to another. Also, lenders do not have to reveal their credit score, nor do they have to reveal the minimum credit score required for the applicant to be accepted. Simply due to this lack of information to the consumer, it is impossible for him or her to know in advance if they will pass a lender's credit scoring requirements.

If the applicant is declined for credit, the lender is also not obliged to reveal the exact reason why. However Industry Associations, such as the Finance and Leasing Association, oblige their members to provide a high level reason. Credit bureau data sharing agreements also require that an applicant declined due to credit bureau data is told that this is the reason and the address of the credit bureau must be provided.

8.2.8.9. United States

In the United States, a credit score is a number based on a statistical analysis of a person's credit files, that in theory represents the creditworthiness of that person, which is the likelihood that people will pay their bills. A credit score is primarily based on credit report information, typically from one of the three major credit bureaus: Experian, Transunion, and Equifax. Income is not considered by the major credit bureaus when calculating a credit score.

There are different methods of calculating credit scores. FICO, the most widely known type of credit score, is a credit score developed by FICO, previously known as Fair Isaac Corporation. It is used by many mortgage lenders that use a risk-based system to determine the possibility that the borrower may default on financial obligations to the mortgage lender. All credit scores have to be subject to availability. The credit bureaus all have their own credit scores: Equifax's Score Power, Experian's PLUS score, and Transunion's credit score, and each also sells the Vantage Score credit score. In addition, many large lenders, including the major credit card issuers, have developed their own proprietary scoring models.

Studies have shown scores to be predictive of risk in the underwriting of both credit and insurance. Some studies even suggest that most consumers are the beneficiaries of lower credit costs and insurance premiums due to the use of credit scores. New credit scores have been developed in the last decade by companies such as Scorelogix, PRBC, L2C, etc., which do not use bureau data to predict creditworthiness. Scorelogix's JSS Credit Score uses a different set of risk factors, such as the borrower's job stability, income, income sufficiency, and impact of economy, in predicting credit risk, and the use of such alternative credit scores is on the rise. These new breed of credit scores are often combined with FICO or bureau scores to improve the accuracy of predictions. Most lenders today use some combination of bureau scores and alternative credit scores to develop a better insight into their borrower's ability to pay. It is widely recognized that FICO is measure of past ability to pay and that's why new credit scores that focus more on future ability to pay are being deployed to enhance credit risk models. L2C offers an alternative credit score that utilises payment histories to determine creditworthiness and many lenders use this score in addition to bureau scores to make lending decisions. Many lenders use Scorelogix's JSS score in addition to bureau scores since the JSS score factors job and income stability to determine if the borrower will have the ability to repay debt in the future. It is estimated that FICO score will remain the dominant score but in all likelihood it will always be used in conjunction with other alternative credit scores which offer new layers of risk insights.

8.3. Borrower Rating

Compared to Credit Rating and Credit Score, Borrower Rating is relatively a new concept after the advent of Basel regulations. To calculate the Credit Risk under IRB, AIRB methods, Borrower Rating is a must. Key features of corporate borrower rating systems:

- Identification of the key drivers of default risk, or proxies for them. A large number of different measures are possible. But these are often slightly different ways of looking at the same issue or set of issues.
- Combination of assessments of these drivers in a way which consistently rank orders borrowers according to their default risk. These may include both entirely objective measures and those which contain subjective assessments. In addition, the rating produced by the basic framework (scorecard) may be adjusted/ over-ridden in order to take account of information which is not, or inadequately, reflected in the scorecard. The inclusion of both forms of subjective elements require controls to ensure that they add value to the process, as opposed to introducing randomness that reduces the ability of the scorecard/ rating system to rank order risk. Success in rank ordering risk, which is reflected in measures of discriminating power, appears to be the primary focus in building Financial Services Authority
- Assignment of a probability of default to the borrowers in each rating grade/ score. Under the IRB approach this is required to be done on a pooled basis for all borrowers in a grade. However the major constraint for corporate ratings is that the relative scarcity and correlated pattern

of defaults means that it is correspondingly difficult to have a high level of confidence in PD estimates put forward. The range of plausible outcomes is very wide.

- The ability of the rating system to be proved by its performance is constrained. This is less of an issue as borrower size decreases and the number of defaults increase. In addition, the measure of PD will vary over time for borrowers of equal risk depending on the "rating philosophy" of the system, i.e. how the PD measure varies due to cyclical factors.
- External measures of default risk are widely used in a number of different ways in order to inform and improve internal measures.

While elements of the above are inter-related, it does therefore seem to us that the key issues to be addressed in a standard for a corporate borrower rating system are:

- What criteria need to be included in the rating assignment?
- Does the rating system have an acceptable rating philosophy?
- What represents adequate discrimination in a rating system? (i.e. properly rank ordering borrowers through assigning them to grades)
- How might the ratings be acceptably transformed into PD estimates?
- What use may be made of external measures of default risk to supplement internal experience?

The main criteria considered to arrive at the Borrower Ratings are:

- Borrower size
- Borrower financial leverage or gearing and debt service capacity
- Borrower profitability
- Borrower liquidity
- Management quality
- Economic and political environment
- Structural features and prospects of the industry in which a borrower operates
- A borrower's competitive position within its industry
- Age of borrower
- A borrower's ability to obtain resources from other sources, such as financial markets and the wider group of which it forms a part – this tends to be a mitigant to the standalone risk.

8.4. Chapter Summary

Credit rating reveals the credit worthiness of an instrument of a corporate. It has to be noted that the credit rating is valid only for one year and has to be revisited again.

Credit Score rates the individual borrowers taking into consideration various parameters like earning capacity, expenditures including dependents, existing loans, repayment pattern, etc. Credit Scores are normally dynamic and keep on changing with every change in any of the parameters.

Borrower rating is rating of borrowers both prospective and existing mainly to calculate the Credit Risk of the banks under Basel compliance. Borrower ratings also vary with every change in any of the parameters.

*****

Chapter 9. Treasury Management

Treasury can be understood as funds of the bank (either surplus or negative). Treasury Management can be understood as "Optimally and profitably managing the funds". Treasury Department is the backbone of a bank. Banks should not keep idle funds and at the same time should not be out of funds for the commitments. Hence Treasury Department has to prudently manage the funds inflow and outflow. The major areas of functions of a Treasury Department of a Bank are highlighted in this chapter.

This chapter cannot claim to be comprehensive about the functions of a Treasury Department, but aims at giving an overview of various functions, concepts and jargons relating to a Banks's treasury department.

9.1. Treasury Jargons

- Cash – Settlement for the deal happens on the same day (Deal day = Value day)
- Tom – Settlement for these deal happens on the next working day from the deal date (T + 1 working day)
- Spot – Settlement for these deal happens on the 2nd working day from the deal date (T + 2 working days)
- Forwards – Any deal with settlement date more than spot deals are called a forward deal
- Counterparty – One of the participants in a financial transaction
- SWIFT - Society for Worldwide Interbank Financial Telecommunication
- RTGS - Real Time Gross Settlement
- Exchange Rate – The price of one currency in relation to another
- FEDAI - Foreign Exchange Dealers' Association of India
- LIBOR - London Inter-Bank Offered Rate
- SIBOR - Yard - Slang for a billion
- MIBOR - Mumbai Inter Bank Offered Rate
- Position – The netted total holdings of a given currency
- Spread - The difference between the bid and offer prices

More treasury related jargons are detailed in Appendix 2.

9.2. Treasury Management

Treasury Management (or treasury operations) includes management of an enterprise's holdings, with the ultimate goal of maximizing the firm's liquidity and mitigating its operational, financial and reputational risk. Treasury Management includes a firm's collections, disbursements, concentration, investment and funding activities. In larger firms, it may also include trading in bonds, currencies, financial derivatives and the associated financial risk management.

Larger banks have whole departments devoted to treasury management and supporting their clients' needs in this area. Until recently, larger banks had the stronghold on the provision of treasury management products and services. However, smaller banks are increasingly launching and/or expanding their treasury management functions and offerings, because of the market opportunity afforded by the recent economic environment (with banks of all sizes focusing on the clients they serve best), availability of (recently displaced) highly-seasoned treasury management professionals, access to industry standard, third-party technology providers' products and services tiered according to the needs of smaller clients, and investment in education and other best practices.

For non-banking entities, the terms *Treasury Management* and *Cash Management* are sometimes used interchangeably, while, in fact, the scope of treasury management is larger (and includes funding and investment activities mentioned above). In general, a company's treasury operations come under the control of the CFO, Vice-President/ Director of Finance or Treasurer, and are handled on a day to day basis by the organisation's treasury staff, controller, or comptroller. The organisation chart of a typical treasury department in a bank would look like:

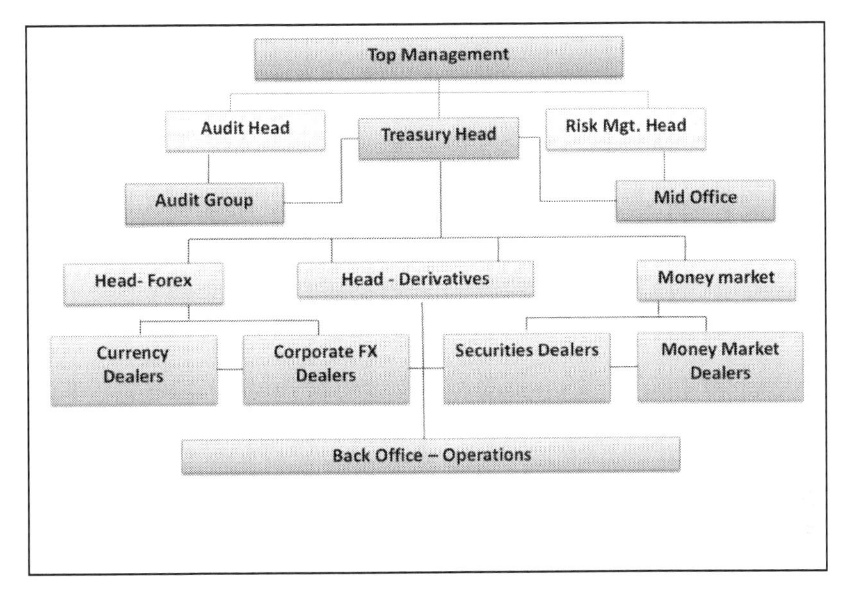

Figure 8 – Treasury Department Organisation Chart

From the outlook of a customer, treasury department will look as:

- Customer who walks into branch for Purchase of Foreign currencies
- Deal is booked by the dealers or Traders in the Trading Room
- The transfer of funds into customer's account by various means like Physical delivery, crediting account of the customer, sending SWIFT/ RTGS

From a bank's perspective there are three departments involved namely:

- Front Office
    - Investment Management
    - Sales & Trading
    - Merchant Banking
- Mid office
    - Research & Strategy
    - Position Keeping
    - P & L Evaluation
    - Risk Management
    - MTM Evaluation
    - Performance Monitoring

- Back office
    - Deal Input Verification
    - Deal Confirmation
    - Settlement
    - Reconciliation
    - Treasury Accounting
    - Documentation
    - Regulatory Reporting
    - Static Data Maintenance

Where does the Treasury get funds from?

- Domestic customers maintaining Local Currency Deposit with the bank
- Deposits in foreign currency
- Imports and Exports

These are the various sources of funds inflows for treasury.

9.3. Treasury Setup

High-level the treasury setup in any bank globally would be:

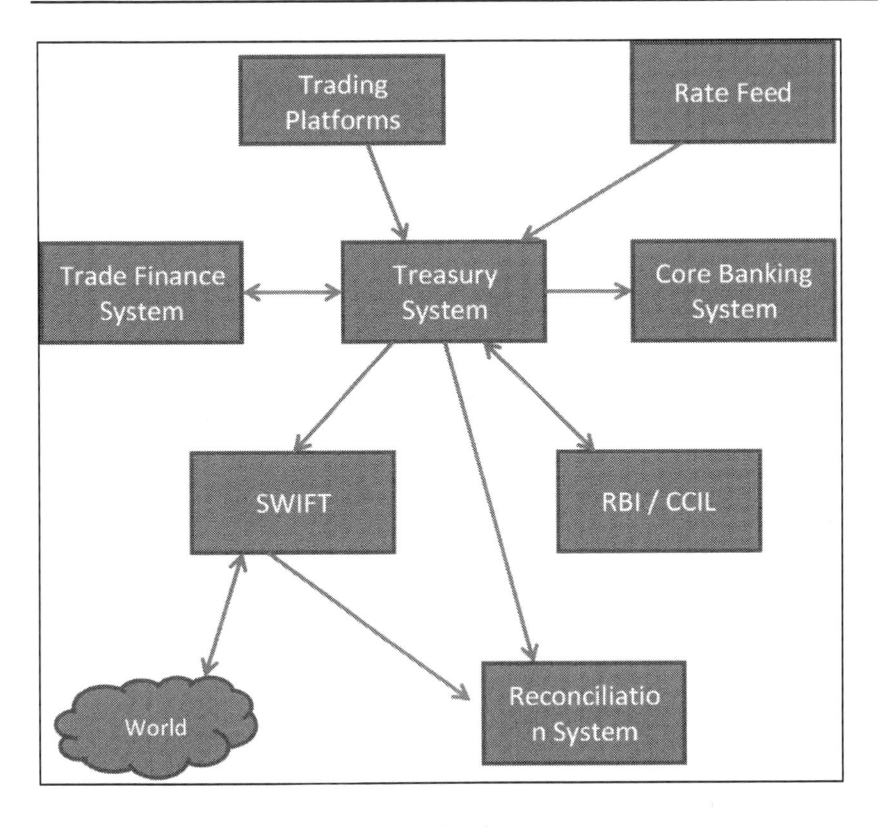

Figure 9 – Standard Treasury Setup

Bank Treasuries may have the following sections/ departments:

- A Fixed Income or Money Market desk that is devoted to buying and selling interest bearing securities
- A Foreign exchange or 'FX' desk that buys and sells currencies
- A Capital Markets or Equities desk that deals in shares listed on the stock market.

In addition the Treasury function may also have a Proprietary Trading desk that conducts trading activities for the bank's own account and capital, an Asset liability management or ALM desk that manages the risk of interest rate mismatch and liquidity; and a Transfer pricing or Pooling function that prices liquidity for business lines (the liability and asset sales teams) within the bank.

Banks may or may not disclose the prices they charge for Treasury Management products, however the Phoenix Hecht Blue Book of Pricing may be a useful source of regional pricing information by product or service.

It is necessary to understand and appreciate the three distinct roles Treasury is expected to play:

- Liquidity Management: Treasury is responsible for managing short-term funds across currencies, and also for complying with reserve requirements (CRR – Cash Reserve Ratio and SLR – Statutory Liquidity Ratio)
- Proprietary Positions: Treasury may trade in currencies, securities and other financial instruments, including derivatives, in order to contribute to Bank's profits
- Risk Management: Treasury will aid Management on one hand and Bank's clients on the other hand, in managing market risk, using derivative instruments

The multiple roles necessitate Treasury to manage an ALM Book for internal risk management, a Merchant Book for client-related currency and derivative transactions, and a Trading Book for managing its proprietary positions. ALM Book also includes traditional role of Treasury in liquidity management.

Though India has a managed exchange rate regime, Rupee exchange rate is effectively a free-float, with minimum intervention by the central bank. In an open economy, exchange rates are further influenced by macro-economic factors like relative inflation, GDP growth rate, stock markets and commodity markets.

More recently, currency futures have also been introduced. Currency futures are being traded in two major exchanges, with fairly good liquidity in 1 to 3 month contracts. Interest rate futures market is also being activated. Regulators are seriously discussing introduction of new products such as credit derivatives, exchange traded options and cross currency futures.

Treasury operates in markets which are almost free of credit risk, and hence requires very little capital allocation. Secondly, the treasury activity is highly leveraged – the risk capital allocated to Treasury may range between 2% to 5% of the size of transactions handled, hence the return on capital is quite high.

Treasury may do transactions similar to the ones done for the customers in forward market – buy forward and sell forward – without investing funds in actual purchase/ sale of currency, known as paired transactions. Interest arbitrage exists only when one of the currencies exchanged is not fully convertible. There is no interest arbitrage (difference in interest rates between two markets) between free currencies, as the forward premium/ discount are equal to the interest rate differentials. The swap is otherwise used to eliminate currency and interest rate mismatches. The swap route is used extensively to convert cash flows arising from principal and interest payments of loans from one currency to another currency, with or without involving actual exchange of funds. Such products fall under the scope of derivatives.

Inter-bank markets are at the forefront of financial markets and are the first to signal any changes in money supply and the resultant liquidity in the system.

9.4. Chapter Summary

The treasury department of a bank is expected to prudently manage the inflow and outflow of funds through Forex market, Domestic Call Money Market and other Investments. Every change in the trends in the market offer newer products and technologies which, of course comes with related risks.

The Recent Trends which challenges the functioning of Treasury Department are:

- Shorter Settlement Cycles like STP (Straight Through Processing)
- Automated Processes
- Understand cost and impact of operation
- Mergers
- Expanding Global Market
- Rapid Technology Change

*****

Chapter 10. Risk Management and Compliance

What is Risk? - *"It is better to be approximately right than precisely wrong"*.

What is Risk Management? - *"Risk Management is asking what might happen the other 1 percent of the time"*.

Banking Enterprise Risk Management is a huge topic on its own and a book of this nature cannot cover it comprehensively. It is attempted to give an idea or overview of the risks and risk management, mainly based on Basel I and II accords. Basel III has already started its presence in bits and pieces and the plan is to make it regulatory by 2019. But it is not considered in this chapter. The risk management in detail including Basel III has been discussed separately by the same author in his book "Banking GRC".

10.1. Risks in Banks

Banks have to manage a galaxy of risks as depicted in the below figure. There is no way that these risks can be avoided. By proper risk management the effect of risks can be minimised, but it can never be avoided.

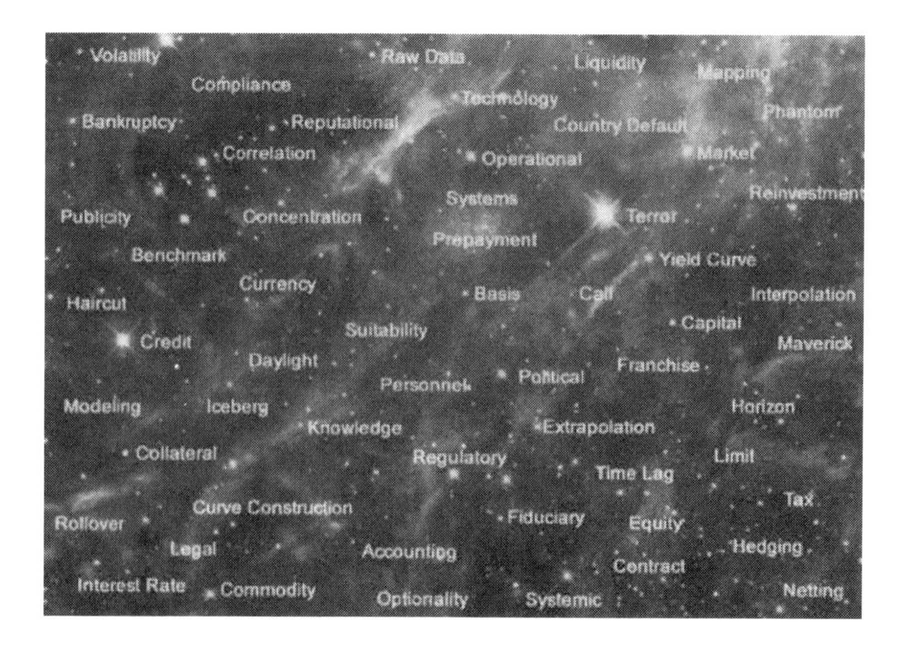

Figure 10 – Galaxy of Risks in Banks

The major risks faced by banks can be classified as in the below landscape;

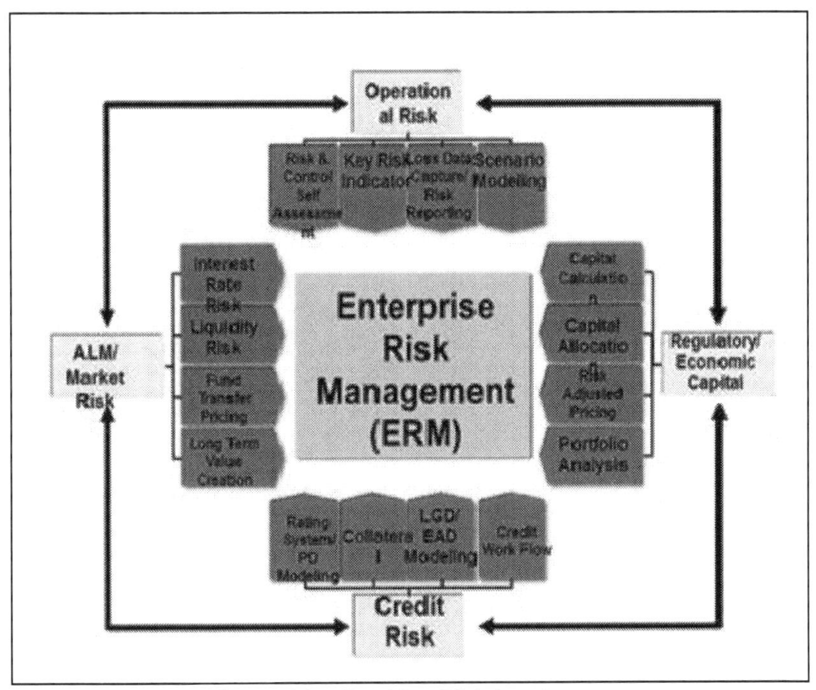

Figure 11 – Banking Risk Landscape

The banking Risks can be classified into three viz.;

- Inherent to the business – on account of business (paid to take)
- Due to management/ mis-management (Paid to Manage)
- On account of operations - avoidable/ mitigatable

The treatments for different risks are different.

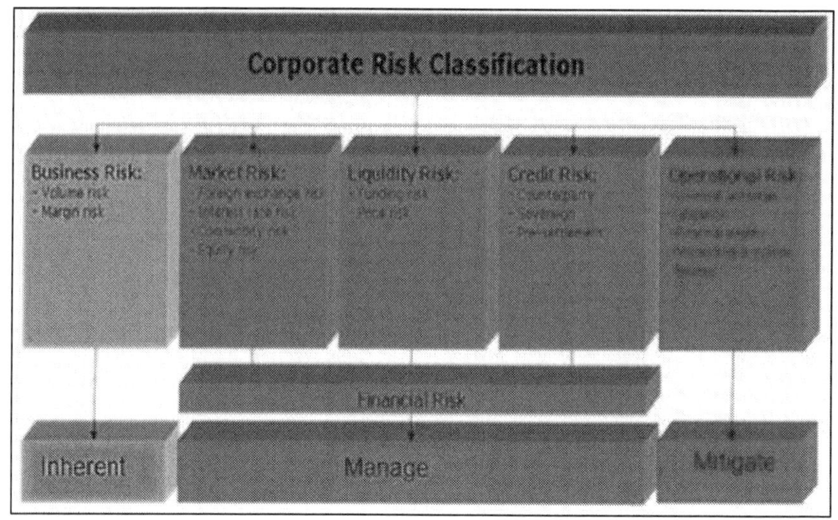

Figure 12 – Banking – Classification of Risks

10.2. Sources of risks

Banks as Financial intermediaries have to do the below tasks inherent to the business and have to face the related risks also;

- Hold assets that are potentially subject to default (Credit Risk)
- Tend to mismatch the maturities of their balance sheets' assets and liabilities (Market Risk and/ or Interest Rate Risk)
- Are exposed to saver withdrawal risk depending on the type of claims they have sold to liability holders (Liquidity Risk)
- Are exposed to market risks due to trading activities
- Are exposed to other risks servicing the customers/ transactions (operational, fraud etc.)

10.3. The nature of Risk and Regulation in banking

What is a Bank?

A **bank** is an institution which holds a banking license, accepts deposits, makes loans, and accepts and issues cheques. In contrast a **financial services company** is an institution that offers to its customers a financial product such as a mortgage, pension, insurance or a bond.

The above definitions highlight the differences between a bank and a financial services company. While a bank is a financial services company, a financial services company is not necessarily a bank. It is important to understand that the regulation of banks is different from that of the financial services industry. Banking regulation is a subset of the overall regulation of financial services.

What is a risk?

The dictionary definition of risk is the chance of disaster or loss. Here, **risk** is defined as the chance of a bad outcome. This implies that risk only relates to situations where a negative outcome could occur and that the likelihood of such an outcome can be estimated.

Two other risk-related terms are important and worth noting:

- **Risk event** is defined as the occurrence of an event that creates the potential for loss (a bad outcome)
- **Risk loss** refers to the losses incurred as a direct or indirect consequence of the risk event. Such losses can be either financial or non-financial.

Most people are familiar with the regulation of non-financial products. Many governments set out guidelines or rules that a company must follow in order to get its product to market. For *example*, cars are subject to product regulation, such as the requirement for seatbelts or airbags. The regulation is there to protect customers.

The financial services industry is also subject to regulations to protect customers and increase confidence in its products. Banks, however, are subject to further regulation. Indeed in the case of banking regulation it is the institution itself that is strictly regulated, not simply the products and services it offers. While it is common to have regulation covering the products or services an industry offers. It is more unusual to have every institution in the industry regulated.

The reason for this high degree of regulation is that the impact of a failure of a bank can have a deep and long-term impact across an entire economy.

While a car manufacturer is subject to product regulation, it is not governed by a regulatory body that regulates every car producer. The car manufacturer may be subject to corporate law and the disclosure requirements of stock exchanges; however it is free to capitalise itself in whatever way, and to whatever extent its management believes is necessary. The company's shareholders provide the only restraint on its management.

This is not the case for banks as they are not free to choose their capital structure. **Capital structure** refers to the way in which a bank finances itself, usually through a combination of equity issues, bonds and loans. The capital structure of a bank is determined by local supervisors who stipulate the minimum capital requirements, as well as the minimum level of liquidity the bank is required to hold, and the type and structure of its lending.

If a bank has sufficient capital it has sufficient financial resources to meet potential losses. If it has sufficient liquidity it has sufficient financial resources to fund its assets and to meet its obligations as they fall due.

Capital structure of a bank – Balance Sheet of Bank A:

Assets	**Amount (USD Million)**	**Risk Weight %**	**RWA (USD Million)**
Domestic government Bonds	100	0	0
Cash	10	0	0
Loans to other banks < 1 year	200	20	40
Loans to MSMEs	390	100	390
Loans to local authorities	200	50	100
Loans to international companies	100	100	100
Total	1,000		630
Liabilities			
Capital	80		
Deposits from Customers	820		
Loans from other banks	100		
Total	1,000		

Notes:

1. RWA = Risk-Weighted Assets
2. Minimum required capital is 8%
3. Bank A does not trade in the markets and hence does not have a trading book
4. Ratio of regulatory capital to RWA = 8% of USD 630 million = USD 50.4 million
5. Comparison of required capital to capital held = USD 50.4 million < USD 80 million

This is a much simplified sample capital structure of a bank. It can be noted that given its asset structure, the supervisor requires the bank to hold minimum capital of USD 50.4 million. The bank is holding USD 80 million, thus surpassing the supervisor's requirement.

Why regulate a bank?

The need for banks to be regulated as institutions has its origins in the risk inherent in the system. Unlike the car industry, banks offer a product that is used by every single commercial and personal customer - money. Thus the failure of a bank, both partially or totally, can affect the entire economy and is referred to as 'systemic risk'.

Systemic risk is the risk that a bank failure could result in damage to the economy out of all proportion to simply the immediate damage to employees, customers and shareholders. While most people may not be familiar with the term systemic risk they do understand what is meant by a 'run on a bank'. This occurs when a bank cannot cover its liabilities; i.e. it does not hold enough cash to pay the depositors who wish to withdraw their funds. The inability to meet liabilities and repay depositors does not necessarily have to be real; it can simply be the result of a perception on the part of its customers.

Example – Run on a Bank

Bank A is rumoured (correctly or not) to have made an extraordinary number of bad loans that have led to losses. This rumour causes the bank's depositors to withdraw their deposits. If Bank A does not hold enough cash, depositors will be unable to withdraw their money, adding to the concern over the bank's stability. This causes more depositors to attempt to withdraw their deposits. Whether the original problem is real or not, the level of withdrawals means Bank A is unable to continue business.

The failure of Bank A causes loans to be foreclosed, as the bank no longer has the deposits to fund them. If Bank A is sufficiently large, its closing (or failure) could have a ripple effect through the local economy; however if it operates globally, the impact would be greater.

The solvency of a bank is a concern not only for its shareholders, customers and employees, but also for those who are in charge of managing the economy as a whole.

Let us look back at the balance sheet given above. This bank has USD 820 million of deposits from customers but only USD 10 million of cash with which to repay the depositors immediately. To raise more cash it could sell its government bond holdings and potentially raise a further USD 100 million. Any attempt to raise further funds would result in loans being sold or foreclosed.

Prior to the 1930s, 'runs' on banks and solvency problems occurred relatively frequently. (The last financial crisis of this nature occurred in the US in 1933 and in the UK in 1957). These led governments to control banks through regulation, ensuring that they were well capitalised and reasonably liquid. Supervisors (usually central banks) sought to ensure that banks could:

- Meet the reasonable level of demand for depositors to be repaid without the need to foreclose on loans
- Sustain a reasonable level of losses as a result of poor lending or cyclical reductions in economic activity, i.e. survive a recession.

The level of capitalisation and liquidity were at first fairly arbitrary, with capital often related to some percentage of loans. In setting the amount of capital as a percentage of some types of loans, it became obvious that there was a 'missing link' in calculating the appropriate capital level for a bank. This missing link is described using the following *example*s;

Bank A only lends to its domestic government, and can always assume that the loans will be repaid.

Bank B only lends to new businesses. It cannot make the same assumption as Bank A as some, possibly many, new businesses might fail.

Clearly the economics of lending to the two groups in the *example* above would be a balance between what could be charged for the loans, commonly referred to as the 'margin', and the losses that would be incurred. Any potential investor in Bank A or Bank B is making a risk/ reward decision based on how much risk each bank is willing to take verses how much reward does it wish to gain. In the *example* above Bank B would seek to earn a higher margin than Bank A as it would incur higher losses. In the case of Bank B, bad debts would unlikely occur at a constant rate as more businesses would default in a recession rather than during periods of economic growth. A bad debt occurs when a bank is unable to recover any of the principal lent to a customer or accrued interest owed. This would cause the bank to suffer variable losses and an erosion of its capital as it is forced to cover each of these losses.

To maintain the expectation that it can survive bad debts, a bank will hold a certain level of funds (capital) from which it would deduct such losses. In the example Bank B would need to hold significantly more capital than Bank A. This is because Bank A pursues a lending policy that, although less rewarding in terms of margin, is more conservative and carries less risk.

From the above *example* it can be seen that the 'missing link' in calculating the appropriate capital level for a bank is the amount of risk it is carrying.

Economic shocks and systemic risk

Despite the best efforts of banks to ensure diversification of their lending portfolios, many still remain heavily exposed to the economic risks of their home market. The economy of a country can be greatly affected by:

- An external shock, be it a natural disaster or a man-made event, and/ or
- Economic mismanagement.

Banks exposed to such an economy may suffer a significant increase in the number of customers defaulting. The increase in the default rate can be attributed to such things as:

- The credit standing of companies affected by the rapid deterioration of the economy
- A significant rise in unemployment levels
- An increase in interest rates.

Many banks will have difficulty in safeguarding themselves from economic shocks in a specific country. However there are certain actions they can take to mitigate the economic effects, including:

- Complying with regulation (including Basel II) which increasingly requires banks to create economic shock scenarios and ensure they hold sufficient capital to protect stakeholders from the effects of such shocks
- Estimating the resulting levels of bad debts and ensuring their businesses are capitalized accordingly.

Risk and capital

The above *example*s clearly demonstrate the relationship between risk and capital. The more risks a business runs the more capital it requires. Banks are required to hold sufficient capital to cover the risks they run. This is known as **capital adequacy**.

It has also become increasingly clear to supervisors that the level of a bank's capital and its ability to support losses from its lending and other activities should be related to the risks of the business it undertakes, i.e. the level of capital should be based on the level of risk (risk-based capital).

The growth of international banking markets in the 1970s and 1980s led to the first significant move in the direction of risk-based capital. Thanks in part to the huge increase in oil prices, countries with large US dollar surpluses needed to recycle those dollars to countries with significant deficits. The result was a dramatic growth in international banking and increased competition. It had become clear to supervisors that international banks needed to ensure they were capitalized against the risks they were running. At the same time lending increasingly took the form of syndicated loan transactions to multinational companies, developing countries and major development projects, all of which represented new areas of lending for many of the banks involved.

Bank Regulation

Basel I – The Basel Committee on Banking Supervision made the first attempt to establish a standardized methodology for calculating the amount of risk based capital a bank would be required to hold when it published the first Basel Capital Accord in 1988.

The first Accord only covered credit risk and the relationship between risk and capital was crude by current standards. A simple set of different multipliers (known as risk weights) for government debt, bank debt and corporate and personal debt was multiplied by an overall 8% target capital ratio.

The Market Risk Amendment

Supervisors in several countries extended the 1988 Accord to make it more risk sensitive. Supervisors then moved quickly to take advantage of the work being undertaken by many banks to manage the risks in their own dealing (trading) operations.

For *example*, to ensure that risks were controlled and priced correctly banks started setting internal capital requirements for their trading desks. The capital requirements were directly related to the risks that the trading desks were running. To do this the banks had to establish a view of the relationship between risk and capital. This view was based on the growing use of finance theory, specifically the historic variability of return from different businesses.
The work undertaken by the banks themselves to manage risks had been given a great deal of impetus as a result of:

- The growth of derivatives markets
- Option pricing models which directly linked the volatility of returns of an underlying market instrument to its price, i.e. risk-based pricing.

The Basel Committee published the Market Risk Amendment to the original Accord in 1996. In addition to creating a simple set of rules for calculating market risk, the Basel Committee encouraged supervisors to focus on appraising the models banks used in risk-based pricing. These are the Value at Risk models (VaR).

Basel II - Following the publication of the Market Risk Amendment the Basel Committee began developing a new Capital Accord which was called Basel II. After much consultation and debate the new Accord was adopted in 2004 and is due for implementation.

Basel II links the capital of banks directly to the risks they carry.

The coverage of market risk in Basel II is substantially unchanged from the 1996 Amendment and its subsequent revisions.

At the same time the coverage of credit risk mirrors, to some extent, the Market Risk Amendment. Banks are encouraged to adopt a model-based approach to credit risk pricing and supervisors are encouraged to appraise these models.

Operational risk is included for the first time and, as with credit risk, a model approach is encouraged, although recognition is given to the lack of industry consensus over the structure of these models.

The Basel II Accord also has provisions for other risks to be taken into account when calculating the risk-based capital of a bank; however these are not covered by a model approach.

Local supervisors will be responsible for implementing Basel II in accordance with their own laws and regulations. The consistent implementation of the new Framework across borders, through enhanced supervision and cooperation, is crucial. Consistent implementation will also be important to avoid confusion over dual reporting to 'home' (where the bank is legally established) and 'host' (where the bank may have branches or subsidiaries) country supervisors.

It is important that each of the major types of risk covered in the new Accord should be understood, as well as their consequences for bank stakeholders and the economy. The major types are:

- Credit risk
- Operational risk
- Market risk
- 'Other' risks.

Credit risk

Credit risk is defined as the risk of losses associated with the possibility that the counterparty will fail to meet the obligations; in other words it is the risk that a borrower won't repay what is owed.

Example*:* Bank A lends mortgages to its personal customers. In doing so it runs the risk that some or all of its customers will fail to pay either the interest on the mortgage or the original sum borrowed.

Operational risk

Operational risk is the risk of loss resulting from inadequate or failed internal processes, people and systems, or from external events.

Market risk

Market risk is defined as the risk of losses in on- and off-balance sheet positions arising from movements in market prices. It is the name given to a group of risks that stem from changes in interest rates, foreign exchange rates and other market determined prices such as those for equities and commodities.

Other risks

Basel II is very specific regarding what is included in `other risks'. It encompasses strategic risk, business risk and reputational risk.

Business risk relates to the competitive position of a bank and to the likelihood of it prospering in changing markets.

Strategic risk is the risk associated with the long term business decisions made by a bank's management.

Reputational risk is not just limited to the reputation of an individual bank; it encompasses the whole sectors of the banking industry. Quantifying the loss resulting from reputational risk can be difficult given the long-term and widespread nature of the effects.

10.4. Effects on supervisors and regulation

Developments in the financial markets and liberalisation of cross-border controls led supervisors, and especially central banks, to consider that although the value of the safety net provided by their lender of last resort function had grown substantially the basis of much of their financial regulation had been weakened.

Prior to the period of financial liberalisation in the 1970s and 1980s financial regulation had focused on:

- The authorisation of financial institutions
- Tightly defining the spheres of permitted activity of different financial institutions
- The definition of balance sheet ratios and requirements such as keeping a certain level of cash deposits with the central bank, or keeping a certain level of assets in domestic government securities.

New approaches to regulation

In this 'new' world prudential supervisors began to look at potential new approaches to regulation, drawing the following conclusions:

- Significant market participants measured their own performance by looking at the return on the risks they took. If the supervisors could create regulatory processes that worked with the markets, they could make regulation both more effective and more relevant to the regulated institutions
- The increase in the globalisation of capital markets greatly increased the need to ensure prudential norms were accepted internationally and implemented consistently
- Regulation was only one part of the solution. The risks of financial intermediation, internationally, depended on such issues as ensuring minimum standards in contract and bankruptcy law, accounting and audit standards and disclosure requirements.

10.5. Chapter Summary

The banking industry is different from other industries in that the failure of a bank, either partial or total, will have an impact on the entire economy; hence bank failure carries 'systemic risk'.
Banks as financial intermediaries are a powerful force for allocating loan capital to enterprises and thus 'employing' the savings of their depositors. If, however, a bank made loans that borrowers could not repay, the insolvency of the bank could lead not only to the destruction of shareholders' equity but to the destruction of depositors' funds as well. This is because a bank is, by its very nature, highly geared.

On account of inherent nature of its business, banks do face a galaxy of risks out of which Credit, Operational and Market Risks are the major ones.

Depending on its size and risk appetite banks do take various management systems. But the maxim is that "Risks cannot be avoided – at the most their impact can be reduced by proper management".

Basel III recommendations are in draft mode and yet to take a final shape.

*****

Chapter 11. Securitisation

Factoring, in Banking, is a financial transaction whereby a bank sells its loans receivable to a third party (called a factor) at a discount.

On the contrary **Securitisation** is a financial practice of pooling various types of contractual debt such as residential mortgages, commercial mortgages, auto loans or credit card debt obligations, etc., and selling said consolidated debt as bonds, pass-through securities, or Collateralized mortgage obligation (CMOs), to various investors. The principal and interest on the debt, underlying the security, is paid back to the various investors regularly. Securities backed by mortgage receivables are called mortgage-backed securities (MBS), while those backed by other types of receivables are asset-backed securities (ABS). Though operationally Factoring and Securitisation are different, both are used by banks as tools for getting immediate liquidity. While Factoring is in vogue for quite some time in global banking industry, Securitisation is practiced only for a couple of decades. Both these tools are in a way used to reduce the credit risk of the banks under Basel II considerations.

11.1. Factoring

In 'advance' factoring, the factor provides financing to the seller of the accounts in the form of a cash 'advance', often 70-85% of the purchase price of the accounts, with the balance of the purchase price being paid, net of the factor's discount fee (or commission) and other charges, upon collection. In 'maturity' factoring, the factor makes no advance on the purchased accounts; rather, the purchase price is paid on or about the average maturity date of the accounts being purchased in the batch. Factoring differs from a bank loan in several ways. The emphasis is on the value of the receivables (essentially a financial asset), whereas a bank focuses more on the value of the borrower's total assets, and often considers, in underwriting the loan, the value attributable to non-accounts collateral owned by the borrower also, such as inventory, equipment, and real property, i.e., matters beyond the credit worthiness of the firm's accounts receivables and of the account debtors (obligors) thereon. Secondly, factoring is not a loan – it is the purchase of a financial asset (the receivable). Third, a nonrecourse factor assumes the "credit risk" that a purchased account will not collect due solely to the financial inability of account debtor to pay. In the United States, if the factor does not assume credit risk on the purchased accounts, in most cases a court will re-characterise the transaction as a secured loan.

The three parties directly involved in Factoring are: the one who sells the receivable, the debtor (the account debtor, or customer of the seller), and the factor. The receivable is essentially a financial asset associated with the debtor's liability to pay money owed to the seller (usually for work performed or goods sold). The seller then sells one or more of its invoices (the receivables) at a discount to the third party, the specialized financial organisation (aka the factor), often, in advance factoring, to obtain cash. The sale of the receivables essentially transfers ownership of the receivables to the factor, indicating the factor obtains all of the rights associated with the receivables. Accordingly, the factor obtains the right to receive the payments made by the debtor for the invoice amount and, in nonrecourse factoring, must bear the loss if the account debtor does not pay the invoice amount due solely to his or its financial inability to pay. Usually, the account debtor is notified of the sale of the receivable, and the factor bills the debtor and makes all collections; however, non-notification factoring, where the client (seller) collects the accounts sold to the factor, as agent of the factor, also occurs. There are three principal parts to 'advance' factoring transaction;

- The advance, a percentage of the invoice face value that is paid to the seller at the time of sale
- The reserve, the remainder of the purchase price held until the payment by the account debtor is made and
- The discount fee, the cost associated with the transaction which is deducted from the reserve, along with other expenses, upon collection, before the reserve is disbursed to the factor's client.

Factoring services have not taken off in India with such a pace as in other Western countries, even though they improve velocity of receivables, thus affording better credit control. Only three important factoring systems have been established, namely, SBI, Canara Bank and SIDBI. Experience of existing factoring companies in India is that average credit period of receivables is cut by more than 25 percent resulting in cost reduction of working capital. The rigorous follow-up by factoring companies also decreases debt delinquency.

11.2. Securitisation

Securitisation is one of the latest financial innovations in the global banking industry. It is still in its nascent stages, with securitised assets as low as about 5% of all debt outstanding. In December 2002, a legal framework was provided in India for securitisation through the Securitisation and Reconstruction of Financial Assets and Enforcement of Security Interest Act, 2002 (SARFAESI). In this Act, the provisions of securitisation have been clubbed with provisions of asset reconstruction and enforcement of security interest. Though these provisions are heterogeneous in nature, one thing that is common to them is that they are related to banks and financial institutions. This new law has introduced certain major changes in the legal framework for transactions in the financial market as under:

- Non-possessory securities are also made enforceable by Banks/ Financial Institutions (FIs). Securities are the documents entitling the holder to specified realisation rights in land, money, stocks, shares, bonds, mortgages, etc. Possessory securities are those securities which are gained by possession. Non- possessory securities refer to those securities which are not in the possession of the title holder, like land, mortgages, etc.
- All mortgages and charges on immovable properties in favour of Banks and FIs are now made enforceable without the intervention of the courts.
- A formal legal framework is provided for securitisation and asset reconstruction transactions.
- Provision is made for setting up a computerised central registry for registration of securitisation, reconstruction and security interest transactions.

In the framework for securitisation, Banks and FIs are not permitted to create special purpose vehicles (SPVs) or special purpose establishments (SPEs) for undertaking such transactions. The law contemplates establishment of a securitisation company or Reconstruction Company and its registration with Reserve Bank of India. Such a company in turn formulates schemes, and sets up (scheme-wise) separate trusts. RBI is required to frame regulations to be complied with and observed by such companies and the trusts to be set up by them. A securitisation company can also act as an asset reconstruction company, and vice versa.

The purpose of securitisation is to avoid mismatch between assets and liabilities of Banks/ FIs. The lending company sells its loans to the investors through the SPV. The company securitizing assets can acquire financial assets from Banks/ FIs, by issuing debentures, bonds or entering into any arrangements with the lenders/ issuers. Once the company takes over the financial assets, it will be treated as lender and secured creditor for all purposes. It may then devise a separate scheme for each of the financial assets taken over. Qualified institutional buyers (QIBs) will invest in such a scheme. The QIBs include FIs, banks, insurance companies, trusts, asset management companies, provident funds, gratuity funds, pension funds and foreign institutional investors (FIIs). The company will issue security receipts to QIBs, which represent undivided interest in such financial assets. The company will realize the financial assets and redeem the investment and payment of returns to QIBs under each scheme. Any disputes among banks, FIs, securitisation or reconstruction companies and QIBs shall be compulsorily referred for conciliation or arbitration under the Arbitration and Conciliation Act, 1996.

11.2.1. Problems and Ambiguities

Some problems and ambiguities relating to securitisation in India are:

- In India, the secondary market for debt, which offers an easy exit route to investors, is still not developed.
- Public sector banks, which are dealing with a huge pool of debts, have not yet looked at these products seriously.
- Trusts and provident funds, which are the major sources of huge funds, have limitations on investment in structured products. Only a number of regulatory changes could help release more funds for investment in these products.
- Though the SARFAESI law has been passed, a number of grey areas still remain:
    - Problems Relating to Income Tax – where there is transfer of income without transfer of assets, the income is chargeable in the hands of the transferor. Exemption from this provision for securitisation is essential. Provisions relating to tax deducted at source also need some clarification
    - Legal Issues – stamp duty is one of the major hindrances to the development of securitisation in India.
- Another important aspect that hinders the growth of securitisation in India is the lack of effective foreclosure laws. The existing foreclosure

laws are not lender-friendly and increase the risks of mortgage-backed securities by making it difficult to transfer property in cases of default.

11.3. Securitisation: The Global Scenario

Securitisation has emerged as one of the dominant means of capital formation throughout the world, and particularly in the US, Canada, Europe, Latin America and South-East Asia. Each year trillions of dollars of securitisation transactions are structured by a wide range of entities like financial institutions, auto financiers, leasing companies, credit card issuers, infrastructure and insurance companies, governments and local authorities.

United States: More than 75% of global securitisation volumes are accounted for by the US. Both institutional and individual investors partake in this vast market. US investors also participate in the securitisation issues of other major markets such as Europe and Japan. The US markets are very liquid, innovative and sophisticated. In the US, the market for CDOs had grown phenomenally from $1bn in 1995 to $234.5bn in 2002. The US securitisation market has grown beyond $5 trillion, providing necessary liquidity to US financial institutions and their customers, both individuals and businesses. SPEs are critical components of this process.

Canada: The securitisation market in Canada is vibrant, fast growing and innovative. It has brought some cutting edge structures into the mechanism of securitisation. The first securitisation of mutual fund fees was done in Canada. Residential mortgages, credit card account receivables, and auto loans and leases make up about 60% of the outstanding asset-backed debt. The other types of assets include equipment leases and loans, commercial mortgages and trade account receivables. The Canadian securitisation market has grown dramatically during the past four to five years. In this period, it increased from $12bn to $76bn including both asset-backed commercial paper and debt, mainly due to entrance of banks into securitisation markets. However, much of the asset-backed debt was in the private placement market until early 1999 when public issues began to pick up.

Europe: UK, France, Spain, Italy and Germany are the major players. The total outstanding volume of European MBS/ ABS is over $130bn of which nearly 50% is accounted for by MBS transactions. With the advent of the

Euro, cross-border transactions are no longer hindered by currency differences.

Asia: Japan's banking system, plagued by a high percentage of non-performing loans, hopes to adopt the securitisation route to partly mitigate the problem of bad loans. With a suitable regulatory framework already in place and market stimulating measures expected to be undertaken by the government, perhaps Japan could also emerge as a major player. One of the most notable issues to emerge from Asian markets in 2000 was the $367m issue maturing in 2009, by Korea Asset Funding Ltd (issuer). It was the first international securitisation of non-performing loans originated by Korea Asset Management Corp (KAMCO). The other Asian countries where significant presence of securitisation is felt include Hong Kong, Thailand and Malaysia.

Latin America: While the region's securitisation markets are less developed than those of North America and Europe, Argentina and many other Latin American countries have been making significant strides recently to develop the legal and financial infrastructure needed. In 2000, the total cross border issuance was $2.6bn, of which 80% comprised future flows. The issuers were from bigger Latin American countries. Mexico maintained the lead with 49% share in the total, followed by Argentina (29%) and Brazil (26%). Latin America continues to move into the secondary stage of securitizing the existing assets that are denominated in local currencies and selling these securities in their domestic capital markets, from its primary stage of cross border future flow issuance. Changes in regulatory, tax, and legal frameworks, and the privatisation of pension systems have been the driving forces in this process.

11.4. Securitisation Process

Asset securitisation in its basic form consists of the pooling of a group of homogenous loans, the sale of these assets to a special purpose company or trust, and the issue by that entity of marketable securities against the pooled assets.

A very high level business process flow is:

- To initiate the securitisation process, a pool of homogenous assets like mortgages, credit card receivables or automobile loans is created.

- The pool is sold to a Special Purpose Vehicle (SPV) which finances the purchase by issuing securities backed by the pool of assets and which are the sole assets of the SPV.
- At this stage, a rating agency is sometimes, involved to analyse the credit quality of the portfolio and structure the transaction.
- To facilitate the securitisation process, a Servicer and a trustee are also normally involved.
- When the securitisation is closed, funds flow from the purchasers of the securities to the Special Purpose Vehicle and from the Special Purpose Vehicle to the Bank.
- The receivables thus securitized are moved off the Balance Sheet of the Bank.

Let us try to understand the process more clearly:

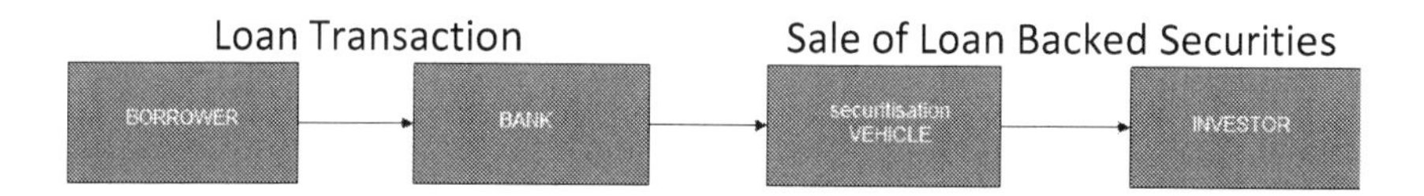

- Bank originates and administers the loan.
- Bank sells loan to securitisation vehicle which issues loan asset backed securities.
- Funding and credit risk of borrower is borne by investor.
- Bank risk is confined to credit risk pre-sale to securitisation vehicle and any underwriting risk on the placement of the loan asset backed securities

A case study – Traditional Securitisation

Stage One:

- Model Bank Ltd. sanctions loans to various Home Loan buyers against mortgage of land and building.

Stage Two:

- Bank decides to sell/ transfer its entire Home Loan outstanding balances of US$ 100 Million.
- All such accounts stand classified as performing (standard) assets.

Stage Three:

- A Special Purpose Entity (SPE) is created by the Bank and Home Loan accounts aggregating US$ 100 million are transferred by way of sale to SPE

Stage Four:

- Model Bank provides guarantee to SPE investors (for the securities) have added comfort of payments.

Stage Five:

- SPE issues transferable and tradable securities with/ without credit enhancement by Model Bank to the investors
- Investors have to make cash payments for purchase of securities covered by underlying assets.

Stage Six:

- Cash received by SPE is passed on to Model Bank after deduction of its fees/ charges.

Final Stage :

- As and when repayments are made by the borrowers to Model Bank – (they are not concerned whether Loan accounts are sold or not, and they are to repay only to Model Bank), the same are passed on to SPE for eventual remittance to the investors of securities.

Figure 13 – Securitisation Process

Operational requirements for Traditional securitisation

- Transferor-Bank must not maintain effective or indirect control over the transferred exposures.
- Assets packaged for securitisation purposes must be legally isolated from the Transferor-Bank by way of sale of assets/ sub participation, etc.
- Opinion from a qualified legal counsel must be obtained before effecting transfer.
- Investor purchasing the securities (of the securitised exposures) would have claim only to the underlying pool of exposures
- No financial obligation from the Transferor – Bank (unless credit enhancement is made available through SPE).
- The transferee must be a legally constituted SPE through a duly stamped/ registered deed.
- The Transferor-Bank has to satisfy the requirement that significant credit risk of the exposure stands transferred to third parties (e.g. covered by deed of guarantee).
- If the aforesaid conditions are complied with, the originator (i.e. Transferor-Bank) will not be required to hold any 'capital' for transferred assets (sold assets).

11.5. Benefits of Securitisation for the Bank

The main benefit from Asset Securitisation is that it enables the Bank to pass the risk of lending on to other parties, thus freeing capital resources to back new lending. Besides, securitisation provides a number of benefits in respect of prudential requirements, asset and liability management and profitability.

11.6. Chapter Summary

Securitisation has already helped banks and corporates to raise more than US$7 trillion globally. It has emerged as one of the most attractive means of capital formation in the US and in Europe as well as in Asia and Latin America. Generally, income-generating assets are securitized. But even the non-performing loans can also be securitized if the risks can be mitigated by several asset diversification and credit enhancement techniques. In Japan, China, Indonesia and Malaysia, securitisation of non-performing loans has picked up greatly.

In India, the SARFAESI law is an extremely important piece of legislation. Implemented in proper spirit, it can provide safe harbour to secured lenders and may enlarge investment in corporate finance. But lack of clarity on some of the issues pertaining to this law and various other issues relating to the taxation matters, high incidence of stamp duties, and lack of investor appetite and understanding of the instrument amongst investors, originators and even rating agencies appear to be some of the reasons for the tardy growth of securitisation.

Though securitisation in India is in a nascent stage, it holds a great promise in the MBS/ ABS areas, particularly for funding resource-starved sectors like infrastructure, power, and housing. There is a lot of scope for further growth in the securitisation of the other assets like credit cards, trade credits, receivables, auto loans and lease receivables. Project finance loans, both performing and non-performing, bonds, and commercial and residential mortgages have also a great future, pursuant to the legislation passed and various other measures being taken by the government to clear the ambiguity in various matters. However, the government and the regulatory authorities in India must realize that the market stimulating measures taken by them to date remain incomplete and that further action will be necessary for the Indian securitisation market to achieve its true potential.

*****

Chapter 12. Islamic Banking

Islamic banking is relatively a new concept – say less than half a century old and is still evolving. Obviously this would be practiced by banks in Islamic countries. There are more grey areas especially when the banks in Islamic countries want to transact with banks in non-Islamic countries. However, let us discuss some concepts being followed in this area.

12.1. Introduction

Modern banking system was introduced into the Muslim countries at a time when they were politically and economically at low ebb, in the late 19th Century. The main banks in the home countries of the imperial powers established local branches in the capitals of the subject countries and they catered mainly to the import export requirements of the foreign businesses. The banks were generally confined to the capital cities and the local population remained largely untouched by the banking system. The local trading community avoided the 'foreign' banks both for nationalistic as well as religious reasons. However, as time went on, it became difficult to engage in trade and other activities without making use of commercial banks. Even then many confined their involvement to transaction activities such as current accounts and money transfers. Borrowing from the banks and depositing their savings with the bank were strictly avoided in order to keep away from dealing in interest which is prohibited by religion.

With the passage of time, however, and other socio-economic forces demanding more involvement in national economic and financial activities, avoiding the interaction with the banks became impossible. Local banks were established on the same lines as the interest-based foreign banks for want of another system and they began to expand within the country bringing the banking system to more local people. As countries became independent the need to engage in banking activities became unavoidable and urgent. Governments, businesses and individuals began to transact business with the banks, with or without liking it. This state of affairs drew the attention and concern of Muslim intellectuals. The story of interest-free or Islamic banking begins here. In the following paragraphs this story has been traced to date and examined as to how far and how successfully the concerns have been addressed. For the benefit of the readers, a list of commonly used Islamic Banking terms is provided in Appendix 1.

12.2. Historical development

It seems that the history of interest-free banking could be divided into two parts. First, when it still remained an idea; second, when it became a reality – by private initiative in some countries and by law in others. The two periods are discussed separately. The last decade has seen a marked decline in the establishment of new Islamic banks and the established banks seem to have failed to live up to the expectations. The literature of the period begins with evaluations and ends with attempts at finding ways and means of correcting and overcoming the problems encountered by the existing banks.

12.2.1. Interest-free banking as an idea

In two decades (1950s and 60s) interest-free banking attracted more attention, partly because of the political interest it created in Pakistan and partly because of the emergence of young Muslim economists. Works specifically devoted to this subject began to appear in this period.

Early seventies saw the institutional involvement. Conference of the Finance Ministers of the Islamic Countries held in Karachi in 1970, the Egyptian study in 1972, First International Conference on Islamic Economics in Mecca in 1976, International Economic Conference in London in 1977 were the result of such involvement. The involvement of institutions and governments led to the application of theory to practice and resulted in the establishment of the first interest-free banks. The Islamic Development Bank, an inter-governmental bank established in 1975, was born of this process.

12.2.2. Interest-free banks in practice

The first private interest-free bank, the Dubai Islamic Bank, was also set up in 1975 by a group of Muslim businessmen from several countries. Two more private banks were founded in 1977 under the name of Faisal Islamic Bank in Egypt and the Sudan. In the same year the Kuwaiti government set up the Kuwait Finance House.

In the ten years since the establishment of the first private commercial bank in Dubai, more than 50 interest-free banks have come into being. Though nearly all of them are in Muslim countries, there are some in Western Europe as well: in Denmark, Luxembourg, Switzerland and the UK.

Many banks were established in 1983 (11) and 1984 (13). The numbers have declined considerably in the following years.

In most countries the establishment of interest-free banking had been by private initiative and were confined to that bank. In Iran and Pakistan, however, it was by government initiative and covered all banks in the country. The governments in both these countries took steps in 1981 to introduce interest-free banking. In Pakistan, effective 1 January 1981 all domestic commercial banks were permitted to accept deposits on the basis of profit-and-loss sharing (PLS). New steps were introduced on 1 January 1985 to formally transform the banking system over the next six months to one based on no interest. From 1 July 1985 no banks could accept any interest bearing deposits, and all existing deposits became subject to PLS rules. Yet some operations were still allowed to continue on the old basis. In Iran, certain administrative steps were taken in February 1981 to eliminate interest from banking operations. Interest on all assets was replaced by a 4 % maximum service charge and by a 4 to 8 % 'profit' rate depending on the type of economic activity. Interest on deposits was also converted into a 'guaranteed minimum profit.' In August 1983 the Usury-free Banking Law was introduced and a fourteen-month change over period began in January 1984. The whole system was converted to an interest-free one in March 1985.

12.3. Current practices

Generally speaking, all interest-free banks agree on the basic principles. However, individual banks differ in their applications. These differences are due to several reasons including the laws of the country, objectives of the different banks, individual bank's circumstances and experiences, the need to interact with other interest-based banks, etc. The salient features common to all banks are discussed below.

12.3.1. Deposit accounts

All the Islamic banks have three kinds of deposit accounts: current, savings and investment.

12.3.2. Current accounts

Current or demand deposit accounts are virtually the same as in all conventional banks. Deposit is guaranteed.

12.3.3. Savings accounts

Savings deposit accounts operate in different ways. In some banks, the depositors allow the banks to use their money but they obtain a guarantee of getting the full amount back from the bank. Banks adopt several methods of inducing their clients to deposit with them, but no profit is promised. In others, savings accounts are treated as investment accounts but with less stringent conditions as to withdrawals and minimum balance. Capital is not guaranteed but the banks take care to invest money from such accounts in relatively risk-free short-term projects. As such lower profit rates are expected and that too only on a portion of the average minimum balance on the ground that a high level of reserves needs to be kept at all times to meet withdrawal demands.

12.3.4. Investment account

Investment deposits are accepted for a fixed or unlimited period of time and the investors agree in advance to share the profit (or loss) in a given proportion with the bank. Capital is not guaranteed.

12.4. Modes of financing

Banks adopt several modes of acquiring assets or financing projects. But they can be broadly categorised into three areas: investment, trade and lending.

12.4.1. Investment financing

This is done in three main ways:

- *Musharaka* where a bank may join another entity to set up a joint venture, both parties participating in the various aspects of the project in varying degrees. Profit and loss are shared in a pre-arranged manner. This is not very different from the joint venture concept. The venture is an independent legal entity and the bank may withdraw gradually after an initial period.
- *Mudarabha* where the bank contributes the finance and the client provides the expertise, management and labour. Profits are shared by both the partners in a pre-arranged proportion, but when a loss occurs the total loss is borne by the bank.

- Financing on the basis of an *estimated rate of return*. Under this scheme, the bank estimates the expected rate of return on the specific project it is financing and provides financing on the understanding that at least that rate is payable to the bank. (Perhaps this rate is negotiable.) If the project ends up in a profit more than the estimated rate the excess goes to the client. If the profit is less than the estimate the bank will accept the lower rate. In case a loss is suffered the bank will take a share in it.

12.4.2. Trade financing

This is also done in several ways. The main ones are:

- *Mark-up* where the bank buys an item for a client and the client agrees to repay the bank the price and an agreed profit later on.
- *Leasing* where the bank buys an item for a client and leases it to him for an agreed period and at the end of that period the lessee pays the balance on the price agreed at the beginning and becomes the owner of the item.
- *Hire-purchase* where the bank buys an item for the client and hires it to him for an agreed rent and period, and at the end of that period the client automatically becomes the owner of the item.
- *Sell-and-buy-back* where a client sells one of his properties to the bank for an agreed price payable now on condition that he will buy the property back after certain time for an agreed price.
- *Letters of credit* where the bank guarantees the import of an item using its own funds for a client, on the basis of sharing the profit from the sale of this item or on a mark-up basis.

12.4.3. Lending

Main forms of Lending are:

- *Loans with a service charge* where the bank lends money without interest but they cover their expenses by levying a service charge. This charge may be subject to a maximum set by the authorities.
- *No-cost loans* where each bank is expected to set aside a part of their funds to grant no-cost loans to needy persons such as small farmers, entrepreneurs, producers, etc. and to needy consumers.
- *Overdrafts* also are to be provided, subject to a certain maximum, free of charge.

12.5. Services

Other banking services such as money transfers, bill collections, trade in foreign currencies at spot rate etc. where the bank's own money is not involved are provided on a commission or charges basis.

12.6. Shortcomings in current practices

The current practices under three categories listed above: deposits, modes of financing (or acquiring assets) and services. There seems to be no problems as far as banking services are concerned. Islamic banks are able to provide nearly all the services that are available in the conventional banks. The only exception seems to be in the case of letters of credit where there is a possibility for interest involvement. However some solutions have been found for this problem – mainly by having excess liquidity with the foreign bank. On the deposit side, judging by the volume of deposits both in the countries where both systems are available and in countries where law prohibits any dealing in interest, the non-payment of interest on deposit accounts seems to be no serious problem. Customers still seem to deposit their money with interest-free banks.

The main problem, both for the banks and for the customers, seems to be in the area of financing. Bank lending is still practised but that is limited to either no-cost loans (mainly consumer loans) including overdrafts, or loans with service charges only. Both these types of loans bring no income to the banks and therefore naturally they are not that keen to engage in this activity much. That leaves us with investment financing and trade financing. Islamic banks are expected to engage in these activities only on a profit and loss sharing (PLS) basis. This is where the banks' main income is to come from and this is also from where the investment account holders are expected to derive their profits from. And the latter is supposed to be the incentive for people to deposit their money with the Islamic banks. And it is precisely in this PLS scheme that the main problems of the Islamic banks lay. Therefore this system has to be more carefully looked into in the following sections.

12.7. The PLS scheme

An overview of the profit and loss sharing scheme of Islamic Banking in three different areas are highlighted below. This shows how Islamic banking is different from conventional banking – where interest is paid or charged.

12.7.1. Savings accounts and capital guarantee

As the name itself indicates the primary aim of the saving account depositor is the safe-keeping of the savings. It is correctly perceived by the conventional banker and he guarantees the return of the deposit *intoto*. The banker also assumes that the depositor will prefer to keep his money with him in preference to another who might also provide the same guarantee, if the depositor is provided an incentive. This incentive is called interest and this interest is made proportional to the amount and length of time it is left with the bank in order to encourage more money brought into the bank and left there for longer periods of time. In addition, the interest rate is fixed in advance so that the depositor and the banker are fully aware of their respective rights and obligations from the beginning. And laws have been enacted to guarantee their enforcement. In Economic theory the interest is often taken to be the 'compensation' the depositors demand and receive for parting with their savings. The fact that the depositors accept the paid interest and that, given other things being equal, they prefer the bank or the scheme which offers the highest interest proves the banker's assumption correct.

The situation is very different in the Islamic banks. Here too the depositor's first aim is to keep his savings in safe custody. Islamic bankers divide the conventional savings account into two categories (alternatively, create a new kind of account):

- Savings Account
- Investment Account

The investment accounts operate fully under the PLS scheme – capital is not guaranteed, neither is there any pre-fixed return. Under the savings account the nominal value of the deposit is guaranteed, but they receive no further guaranteed returns. Banks may consider funds under the savings accounts too as part of their resources and use it to create assets. This is theory. In practice, however, the banks prefer, encourage and emphasise the investment accounts. This is because since their assets operate under the PLS scheme they might incur losses on these assets which they cannot pass onto the savings accounts depositors on account of the capital guarantee on these accounts. In the process the first aim of the depositor is pushed aside and the basic rule of commercial banking – capital guarantee – is broken.

It is suggested that all Islamic banks guarantee the capital under their savings accounts. This will satisfy the primary need and expectation of an important section of the depositors and, in Muslim countries where both Islamic and conventional banks co-exist, will induce more depositors to bank with the Islamic banks. At the same time, it will remove the major objection to establishing Islamic banks in non-Muslim countries.

12.7.2. Loans with a service charge

The problems of the Islamic banks arise from their need to acquire their assets under the PLS scheme. A simple solution does, in fact, already exist in the current theories of Islamic banking. It need only be pointed out and acted upon. There are three different viz. Iranian, Pakistani and the Siddiqi models in this regard.

All three models provide for loans with a service charge. Though the specific rules are not identical, the principle is the same. It is suggested that the funds in the deposit accounts (current and savings) be used to grant loans (short- and long-term) with a service charge. By doing this the Islamic banks will be able to provide all the loan facilities that conventional banks provide while giving capital guarantee for depositors and earning an income for themselves. Furthermore, and it is important, they can avoid all the problems. This would also remove the rest of the obstacles in opening and operating Islamic banks in non-Muslim countries.

The bonus for the borrowers is that the service charge levied by the Islamic banks will necessarily be less than the interest charged by conventional banks.

The existing relevant rules in the three models:

Model 1 – The Iranian model provides for *Gharz-al hasaneh* whose definition, purpose and operation are given in Articles 15, 16 and 17 of Regulations relating to the granting of banking facilities:

Article 15 – Gharz-al-hasaneh is a contract in which one (the lender) of the two parties relinquishes a specific portion of his possessions to the other party (the borrower) which the borrower is obliged to return to the lender in kind or, where not possible, its cash value.

Article 16 – The banks shall set aside a part of their resources and provide Gharz-al-hasaneh for the following purposes:

- To provide equipment, tools and other necessary resources so as to enable the creation of employment, in the form of co-operative bodies, for those who lack the necessary means;
- To enable expansion in production, with particular emphasis on agricultural, livestock and industrial products;
- To meet essential needs.

Article 17 – The expenses incurred in the provision of Gharz-al-hasaneh shall be, in each case, calculated on the basis of the directives issued by the Central bank and collected from the borrower.

Model 2 – In Pakistan, permissible modes of financing include:

Financing by lending:

- Loans not carrying any interest on which the banks may recover a service charge not exceeding the proportionate cost of the operation, excluding the cost of funds and provisions for bad and doubtful debts. The maximum service charge permissible to each bank will be determined by the State Bank from time to time.
- Qard-e-hasana loans given on compassionate grounds free of any interest or service charge and repayable if and when the borrower is able to pay.

Model 3 – Siddiqi has suggested that 50 percent of the funds in the 'deposit' (i.e. current and savings) accounts be used to grant short-term loans. A fee is to be charged for providing these loans:

An appropriate way of levying such a fee would be to require prospective borrowers to pay a fixed amount on each application, regardless of the amount required, the term of the loan or whether the application is granted or rejected. Then the applicants to whom a loan is granted may be required to pay an additional prescribed fee for all the entries made in the banks registers. The criterion for fixing the fees must be the actual expenditure which the banks have incurred in scrutinising the applications and making decisions, and in maintaining accounts until loans are repaid.

These fees should not be made a source of income for the banks, but regarded solely as a means of maintaining and managing the interest-free loans.

It is clear from the above that all three models agree on the need for having cash loans as one mode of financing, and that this service should be paid for by the borrower. Though the details may vary, all seem to suggest that the charge should be the absolute cost only. It can be suggested that a percentage of this absolute cost be added to the charge as a payment to the bank for providing this service. This should enable an Islamic bank to exist and function independently of its performance in it's PLS operations.

12.7.3. Investment under PLS scheme

The idea of participatory financing introduced by the Islamic banking movement is a unique and positive contribution to modern banking. However, as seen earlier, by making the PLS mode of financing the main (often almost the only) mode of financing the Islamic banks have run into several difficulties. If, as suggested in the previous section, the Islamic banks would provide all the conventional financing through lending from their deposit accounts (current and savings), it will leave their hands free to engage in this responsible form of financing innovatively, using the funds in their investment accounts. They could then engage in genuine *Mudaraba* financing. Being partners in an enterprise they will have access to its accounts, and the problems associated with the non-availability of accounts will not arise.

12.8. Problems in implementing the PLS scheme

Several schools of thought were put forth, with varying degrees of success, that Islamic Banking based on the concept of profit and loss sharing (PLS) is theoretically superior to conventional banking from different angles. However from the practical point of view things do not seem that rosy concerning everyone. In the over half-a-decade of full-scale experience in implementing the PLS scheme the problems have begun to show up. Some of the major difficulties in different areas are:

12.8.1. Financing

There are four main areas where the Islamic banks find it difficult to finance under the PLS scheme:

- Participating in long-term low-yield projects
- Financing the small businessman
- Granting non-participating loans to running businesses
- Financing government borrowing

12.8.1.1. Long-term projects

Less than 10 % of the total assets go into medium and long-term investment. Admittedly, the banks were unable or unwilling to participate in long-term projects. The main reason is the need to participate in the enterprise on a PLS basis, which involves time consuming complicated assessment procedures and negotiations, requiring expertise and experience. There are no commonly accepted criteria for project evaluation based on PLS partnerships. Each single case has to be treated separately with utmost care and each has to be assessed and negotiated on its own merits. Other obvious reasons are:

- Such investments tie up capital for very long periods, unlike in conventional banking where the capital is recovered in regular instalments almost right from the beginning, and the uncertainty and risk are that much higher
- The longer the maturity of the project, the longer it takes to realise the returns and the banks therefore cannot pay a return to their depositors as quick as the conventional banks can.

Thus it is no wonder that the banks gave lesser priority to such investments.

12.8.1.2. Small businesses

Small scale businesses form a major part of a country's productive sector. Besides, they form a greater number of the banks' clientele. Yet it seems difficult to provide them with the necessary financing under the PLS scheme, even though there is excess liquidity in the banks.

Given the comprehensive criteria to be followed in granting loans and monitoring their use by banks, small-scale enterprises have, in general encountered greater difficulties in obtaining financing than their large-scale counterparts in the Islamic countries. This has been particularly relevant for the construction and service sectors, which have large share in the gross domestic product (GDP). The service sector is made up of many small producers for whom the banking sector has not been able to provide sufficient financing. Many of these small producers, who traditionally were able to obtain interest-based credit facilities on the basis of collateral, are now finding it difficult to raise funds for their operations.

12.8.1.3. Running businesses

Running businesses frequently need short-term capital as well as working capital and ready cash for miscellaneous on-the-spot purchases and sundry expenses. This is the daily reality in the business world. The PLS scheme is not geared to cater to this need. Even if there is complete trust and exchange of information between the bank and the business, it is nearly impossible or prohibitively costly to estimate the contribution of such short-term financing on the return of a given business. Neither is the much used mark-up system suitable in this case. It looks unlikely to be able to arrive at general rules to cover all the different situations.

Added to this is the delay involved in authorising emergency loans. Often the clients need to have quick access to fresh funds for the immediate needs to prevent possible delays in the project's implementation schedule. According to the set regulations, it is not possible to bridge-finance such requirements and any grant of financial assistance must be made on the basis of the project's appraisal to determine type and terms and conditions of the scheme of financing.

12.8.1.4. Government Borrowing

In all countries the Government accounts for a major component of the demand for credit – both short-term and long-term. Unlike business loans these borrowings are not always for investment purposes, nor for investment in productive enterprises. Even when invested in productive enterprises they are generally of a longer-term type and of low yield.

Continued borrowing on a fixed rate basis by the Government would inevitably index bank charges to this rate than to the actual profits of borrowing entities.

12.8.2. Legislation

Existing banking laws do not permit banks to engage directly in business enterprises using depositors' funds. But this is the basic asset acquiring method of Islamic banks. Therefore new legislation and/ or government authorisation are necessary to establish such banks. In Iran a comprehensive legislation was passed to establish Islamic banks. In Pakistan the Central Bank was authorised to take the necessary steps. In other countries either the banks found work-around ways of using existing regulations or were given special accommodation. In all cases government intervention or active support was necessary to establish Islamic banks working under the PLS scheme.

In spite of this, there is still need for further auxiliary legislation in order to fully realise the goals of Islamic banking.

Iran and Pakistan are countries committed to ridding their economies of *riba* and have made immense strides in towards achieving it. Yet there are many legal difficulties still to be solved as has been seen above. In other Muslim countries the authorities actively or passively participate in the establishment of Islamic banks on account of their religious persuasion. Such is not the case in non-Muslim countries. Here establishing Islamic banks involves conformation to the existing laws of the concerned country which generally are not conducive to PLS type of financing in the banking sector.

12.8.3. Re-training of staff

As one can easily expect, the bank staff will have to acquire many new skills and learn new procedures to operate the Islamic banking system. This is a time consuming process, which is aggravated by two other factors. One, the sheer number of persons that need to be re-trained and, two, the additional staff that need to be recruited and trained to carry out the increased work.

Principles are still to be laid down and techniques and procedures evolved to carry them out. It is only after the satisfactory achievement of these that proper training can begin. This delay and the resulting confusion appear to be among the main reasons for the banks to stick to modes of financing that are close to the familiar interest-based modes.

12.8.4. Other Limitations

Among the other disincentives from the borrower's point of view are the need to disclose his accounts to the bank if he were to borrow on the PLS basis and the fear that eventually the tax authorities will become wise to the extent of his business and the profits. Several writers have lashed out at the lack of business ethics among the business community, but that is a fact of life at least for the foreseeable future. There is a paucity of survey or case studies of clients to see their reaction to current modes of financing. As such the bankers are not aware of further disincentives that might be there.

12.8.5. Accounts

When a business is financed under the PLS scheme it is necessary that the actual profit/ loss made using that money be calculated. Though no satisfactory methods have yet been devised, the first requirement for any such activity is to have the necessary accounts. On the borrowers' side there are two difficulties:

- Many small-time businessmen do not keep any accounts, leave alone proper accounts. The time and money costs will cut into his profits. Larger businesses do not like to disclose their real accounts to anybody.
- On the banks' side the effort and expense involved in checking the accounts of many small accounts is prohibitive and will again cut into their own share of the profits.

Thus both sides would prefer to avoid having to calculate the actually realised profit/ loss.

12.8.6. Excess liquidity

Presence of excess liquidity is reported in nearly all Islamic banks. This is not due to reduced demand for credit but due to the inability of the banks to find clients willing to be funded under the new modes of financing. Some of these difficulties are mentioned above under the head 'Financing'. Here the situation is that there is money available on the one hand and there is need for it on the other but the new rules stand in the way of bringing them together. This is a very strange situation – especially in the developing Muslim countries where money is at a premium even for ordinary economic activities, leave alone development efforts. Removal of riba was expected to ease such difficulties, not to aggravate the already existing ones.

12.8.7. Islamic banking in non-Muslim countries

The modern commercial banking system in nearly all countries of the world is mainly evolved from and modelled on the practices in Europe, especially that in the United Kingdom. The philosophical roots of this system revolve around the basic principles of capital certainty for depositors and certainty as to the rate of return on deposits. In order to enforce these principles for the sake of the depositors and to ensure the smooth functioning of the banking system Central Banks have been vested with powers of supervision and control. All banks have to submit to the Central Bank rules. Islamic banks which wish to operate in non-Muslim countries have some difficulties in complying with these rules.

12.8.8. Certainty of capital and return

While the conventional banks guarantee the capital and rate of return, the Islamic banking system, working on the principle of PLS, cannot, by definition, guarantee any fixed rate of return on deposits. Many Islamic banks do not guarantee the capital either, because if there is a loss it has to be deducted from the capital. Thus the basic difference lies in the very roots of the two systems. Consequently countries working under conventional laws are unable to grant permission to institutions which wish to operate under the PLS scheme to function as commercial banks.

12.8.9. Supervision and control

One other major concern is the Central Bank supervision and control. This mainly relates to liquidity requirements and adequacy of capital. These in turn depend on an assessment of the value of assets of the Islamic banks.

It is evident then that even if there is a desire to accommodate the Islamic system, the new procedures that need be developed and the modifications that need be made to existing procedures are so large that the chances of such accommodation in a cautious sector such as banking is very remote indeed. Any relaxation of strict supervision is precluded because should an Islamic bank fail it would undermine the confidence in the whole financial system, with which it is inevitably identified.

12.9. Core Banking System – Islamic Banking

While Islamic Banking as a practice is still evolving, there is another dimension to it. For want of clear guidelines, concepts and logic no core banking system product vendor has ventured into developing a software product completely catering to the Islamic Banking needs. (Most of the product vendors claim that they have a module for Islamic banking, but no-one is sure how much it covers). Needless to say, all these mean, in the days to come, even application software meant for banks need to reckon the Islamic Code.

12.10. Chapter Summary

People have needs – food, clothes, houses, machinery, services; the list is endless. Entrepreneurs perceive these needs and develop ways and means of catering to them. They advertise their products and services, people's expectations are raised and people become customers of the entrepreneur. If the customers' needs are fulfilled according to their expectations they continue to patronise the entrepreneur and his enterprise flourishes. Otherwise his enterprise fails and people take to other entrepreneurs.

Banks too are enterprises; they cater to peoples' needs connected with money – safe-keeping, acquiring capital, transferring funds etc. The fact that they existed for centuries and continue to exist and prosper is proof that their methods are good and they fulfil the customers' needs and expectations. Conventional commercial banking system as it operates today is accepted in all countries except the Islamic world where it is received with some reservation. The reservation is on account of the fact that the banking operations involve dealing in interest which is prohibited in Islam. Conventional banks have ignored this concern on the part of their Muslim clientele. Muslims patronised the conventional banks out of necessity and, when another entrepreneur – the Islamic banker – offered to address their concern many Muslims turned to him. The question is: has the new entrepreneur successfully met their concerns, needs and expectations? If not he may have to put up his shutters!

Broadly speaking, banks have three types of different customers: depositors, borrowers and seekers of bank's other services such as money transfer. Since services do not generally involve dealing in interest Muslims have no problem transacting such businesses with conventional banks;

neither do Islamic banks experience any problems in providing these services. Among the depositors there are current account holders who too, similarly, have no problems. It is the savings account holders and the borrowers who have reservations in dealing with the conventional banks. In the following paragraphs discuss how well the Islamic banks have succeeded in addressing their customers' special concern.

With only minor changes in their practices, Islamic banks can get rid of all their cumbersome, burdensome and sometimes doubtful forms of financing and offer a clean and efficient interest-free banking. All the necessary ingredients are already there. The modified system will make use of only two forms of financing – loans with a service charge and *Mudaraba* participatory financing – both of which are fully accepted by all Muslim writers on the subject.

Such a system will offer an effective banking system where Islamic banking is obligatory and a powerful alternative to conventional banking where both co-exist. Additionally, such a system will have no problem in obtaining authorisation to operate in non-Muslim countries.

Participatory financing is a unique feature of Islamic banking, and can offer responsible financing to socially and economically relevant development projects. This is an additional service Islamic banks offer over and above the traditional services provided by conventional commercial banks.

*****

Chapter 13. Banking Landscape

The facet of the entire banking operation has undergone a drastic revolution – thanks to Western Banks and Core Banking Systems. It is primarily classified into; Front Office, Mid Office and Back Office functions.

13.1. Emerging Economic Scene

The banking system is the lifeline of the economy. The changes in the economy get mirrored in the performance of the banking industry.

The ability of the banking system in its present structure to make available investible resources to the potential investors in the forms and tenors that will be required by them in the coming years, that is, as equity, long term debt and medium and short-term debt would be critical to the achievement of plan objectives. The gap in demand and supply of resources in different segments of the financial markets has to be met and for this, smooth flow of funds between various types of financial institutions and instruments would need to be facilitated. Financing of infrastructure projects is a specialised activity and would continue to be of critical importance in the future. After all, a sound and efficient infrastructure is a sine qua non for sustainable economic development.

13.2. Banking Operations – Different Perspective

Wherever direct interaction with the customer is involved those operations can be considered as Front office. Mid-office generally validates the front office functions like approval, etc. Back Office functions take care of day-end operations, report generation, routine back-up, etc. There is one more division as support – admin jobs, testing, purchase, etc., normally non-banking related operations. The below diagram gives an overview of various front, mid, back office and support functions.

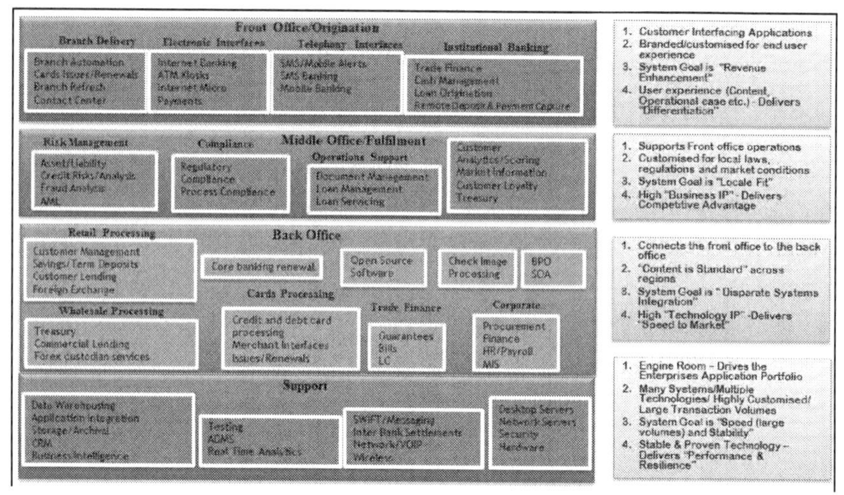

Figure 14 – Banking Landscape

Banking is not just accepting deposits and lending. There are many more functions like Treasury Management, Risk Management, Customer Relationship Management, etc. The author had interacted with many officials of various banks, in different countries both developing and developed. All of them unanimously were of same relaxed opinion that once Core Banking System is implemented for the whole of the bank then the automation is complete. But the author scared them by saying that it is only the beginning and there is lot more to act upon. To stress this point the below diagram illustrates the operations around Core Banking:

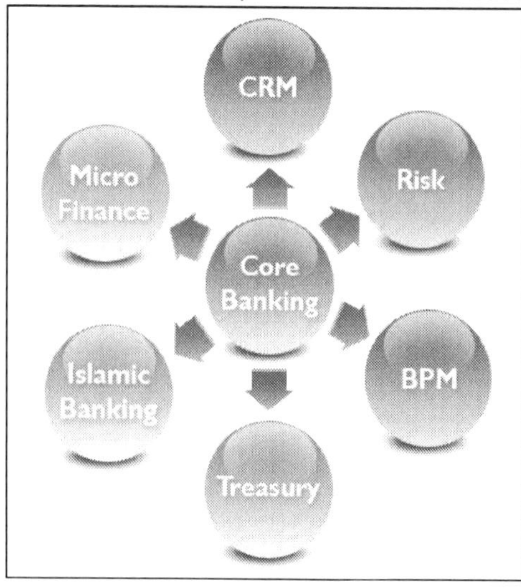

Figure 15 – Around Core Banking

While most of these areas are out of scope of this book; this would give an idea that banking encompasses much more than what is perceived. However, the areas like Islamic Banking and CRM are discussed in other chapters to provide completeness and to make the readers to get an idea of the current trends in the Retail Banking segment. This chapter was aimed at to have a wholesome view of different domains of the Banking industry.

13.3. Dependency on Technology

It is a known factor that the Banking system is globally competitive. To survive in this market, the players will have to be financially strong and operationally efficient. Capital would be a key factor in building a successful institution. The banking system will improve competitiveness through a process of consolidation, either through mergers and acquisitions or through strategic alliances.

Technology would be the key to the competitiveness of banking system. Indian players will keep pace with global leaders in the use of banking technology. In such a scenario, on-line accessibility will be available to the customers from any part of the globe; 'Anywhere' and 'Anytime' banking will be realised truly and fully. At the same time 'brick and mortar' banking will co-exist with 'click' banking to cater to the specific needs of different customers.

Banking system is playing a crucial role in the socio-economic development of the country. The system will continue to be sensitive to the growth and development needs of all the segments of the society.

The banking system that will evolve will be transparent in its dealings and adopt global best practices in accounting and disclosures driven by the motto of value enhancement for all stakeholders.

The banking industry in developing countries like India is moving gradually from a regulated environment to a deregulated market. The market developments kindled by liberalisation and globalisation have resulted in changes in the intermediation role of banks. The pace of transformation has been more significant in recent times with technology acting as a catalyst. While the banking system has done fairly well in adjusting to the new market dynamics, greater challenges lie ahead. Financial sector would be opened up for greater international competition under World Trade

Organisation. Banks will have to gear up to meet stringent prudential capital adequacy norms under Basel II (Basel III is already drafted and soon be adopted). In addition to WTO and Basel II, the Free Trade Agreements (FTAs) such as with Singapore, may have an impact on the shape of the banking industry. Banks will also have to cope with challenges posed by technological innovations in banking. Banks need to prepare for the changes.

13.4. Future Landscape of Banking

Liberalisation and de-regulation processes, in some of the developing countries like India, have made a sea change in the banking system. From a totally regulated environment, the system is moving gradually into a market driven competitive system. The move towards global benchmarks has been, by and large, calibrated and regulator driven. The pace of changes gained momentum in the last decade. Globalisation would gain greater speed in the coming years particularly on account of expected opening up of financial services under WTO. Four trends change the banking industry world over, viz.:

- Consolidation of players through mergers and acquisitions
- Globalisation of operations
- Development of new technology and
- Universalisation of banking

With technology acting as a catalyst, great changes can be expected in the banking scene in the coming years.

The traditional banking functions would give way to a system geared to meet all the financial needs of the customer. The emergence of highly varied financial products, which are tailored to meet specific needs of the customers in the retail as well as corporate segments, can be visualised. The advent of new technologies could see the emergence of new financial players doing financial intermediation. The conventional definition of banking is undergoing complete vicissitudes.

The competitive environment in the banking sector is likely to result in individual players working out differentiated strategies based on their strengths and market niches. For example, some players might emerge as specialists in mortgage products, credit cards etc., whereas some may choose to concentrate on particular segments of business system, while outsourcing all other functions. Some other banks may concentrate on industrial segments or high net worth individuals by providing specially tailored services beyond traditional banking offerings to satisfy the needs of customers they understand better than a more generalist competitor.

Retail lending will receive greater focus. Banks would compete with one another to provide full range of financial services to this segment. Banks would use multiple delivery channels to suit the requirements and tastes of customers. While some customers might value relationship banking (conventional branch banking), others might prefer convenience banking (e-banking).

In the midst of all the advancements, one of the concerns is quality of bank lending. Most significant challenge before banks is the maintenance of rigorous credit standards, especially in an environment of increased competition for new and existing clients. **Experience has shown us that the worst loans are often made in the best of times.**

Structure and ownership pattern would undergo changes. There would be greater presence of international players in any developing country's banking system. Mergers and acquisitions would gather momentum as managements will strive to meet the expectations of stakeholders.

Corporate governance in banks and financial institutions would assume greater importance in the coming years and this will be reflected in the composition of the Boards of Banks.

13.5. Product Innovation and Process Re-Engineering

With increased competition in the banking Industry, the net interest margin of banks has come down over the last one decade. Liberalisation with Globalisation will see the spreads narrowing further as in the case of banks operating in developed countries. Banks will look for fee-based income to fill the gap in interest income. Product innovations and process re-engineering will be the order of the day. The changes will be motivated by the desire to meet the customer requirements and to reduce the cost and improve the efficiency of service. All banks will therefore go for rejuvenating their costing and pricing to segregate profitable and non-profitable business. The new paradigm in the coming years will be **cost = revenue - profit**.

As banks strive to provide value added services to customers, the market will see the emergence of strong investment and merchant banking entities. Product innovation and creating brand equity for specialised products will decide the market share and volumes. New products on the liabilities side such as Forex linked deposits; investment-linked deposits, etc. are likely to be introduced, as investors with varied risk profiles will look for better yields. There will be more and more of tie-ups between banks, corporate clients and their retail outlets to share a common platform to shore up revenue through increased volumes.

Banks will increasingly act as risk managers to corporate and other entities by offering a variety of risk management products like options, swaps and other aspects of financial management in a multi-currency scenario. Banks will play an active role in the development of derivative products and will offer a variety of hedge products to the corporate sector and other investors. For example, Derivatives in emerging futures market for commodities would be an area offering opportunities for banks. As the integration of markets takes place internationally, sophistication in trading and specialised exchanges for commodities will expand. As these changes take place, banking will play a major role in providing financial support to such exchanges, facilitating settlement systems and enabling wider participation.

13.6. Chapter Summary

On account of technological advancement, globalisation, liberalisation, etc., the banking industry in developing countries is undergoing a manifestation.

- Banks will have to adopt global standards in capital adequacy, income recognition and provisioning norms.
- Risk management setup in Banks will need to be strengthened.
- Benchmark standards could be evolved.
- Payment and settlement system will have to be strengthened to ensure transfer of funds on real time basis eliminating risks associated with transactions and settlement process.
- Regulatory set-up will have to be strengthened, in line with the requirements of a market-led integrated financial system
- Banks will have to adopt best global practices, systems and procedures.

- Banks may have to evaluate on an ongoing basis, internally, the need to effect structural changes in the organisation. This will include capital restructuring through mergers/ acquisitions and other measures in the best business interests.
- There should be constant and continual upgradation of technology in the Banks, benefiting both the customer and the bank. Banks may enter into partnership among themselves for reaping maximum benefits, through consultations and coordination with reputed IT companies.
- The skills of bank staff should be upgraded continuously through training. In this regard, the banks may have to relook at the existing training modules and effect necessary changes, wherever required. Seminars and conferences on all relevant and emerging issues should be encouraged.
- Banks will have to set up Research and Market Intelligence units within the organisation, so as to remain innovative, to ensure customer satisfaction and to keep abreast of market developments. Banks will have to interact constantly with the industry bodies, trade associations, farming community, academic/ research institutions and initiate studies, pilot projects, etc. for evolving better financial models.

*****

Chapter 14. CRM and Bank Marketing

Today, many businesses including banks realise the importance of Customer Relationship Management (CRM) and its potential to help them acquire new customers, retain existing ones and maximize their lifetime value. At this point, close relationship with customers will require a strong coordination between IT and marketing departments to provide a long-term retention of selected customers. The advent of Call Centers for banks is mainly the first step towards customer relationship manager and marketing. CRM is completely dependent on technology concepts like Data Warehouse, Data Mining, Analytics, etc.
This chapter aims at providing an overview of CRM in banks and tries to stress on marketing in banks to survive in the competitive market. At the same time care is taken not to divert the contents of this chapter as more technical.

14.1. Customer Relationship Management in Banks

CRM is a sound business strategy to identify the bank's most profitable customers and prospects, and devote time and attention to expanding account relationships with those customers through individualised marketing, reprising, discretionary decision making, and customised service-all delivered through the various sales channels that the bank uses.

In literature, many definitions were given to describe CRM. The main difference among these definitions is technological and relationship aspects of CRM. Some schools from marketing background emphasize technological side of CRM while the others consider IT perspective of CRM. From marketing aspect, CRM is defined as "a combination of business process and technology that seeks to understand a company's customers from the perspective of who they are, what they do, and what they are like". Technological definition of CRM was given as "the market place of the future is undergoing a technology-driven metamorphosis". Consequently, IT and marketing departments must work closely to implement CRM efficiently. Meanwhile, implementation of CRM in banking sector focused on the evaluation of the critical satisfaction dimensions and the determination of customer groups with distinctive preferences and expectations in the private bank sector. Specifically the customer relationships of new technology-based firms were interested in total sales activities, both volume-related and non-volume related. They also developed a modification of the standard data envelope analysis (DEA) structure using goal programming concepts that yields both a sales and service measures.

14.1.1. Objectives of CRM in Bank

The idea of CRM is that it helps businesses use technology and human resources gain insight into the behavior of customers and the value of those customers. If it works as hoped, a business can provide better customer service, make call centers more efficient, cross sell products more effectively, help sales staff close deals faster, simplify marketing and sales processes, discover new customers, and increase customer revenues. It doesn't happen by simply buying software and installing it. For CRM to be truly effective an organisation must first decide what kind of customer information it is looking for and it must decide what it intends to do with that information. For example, many banks keep track of customers' life stages in order to market appropriate banking products to them at the right time to fit their needs. Next, the organisation must look into all of the different ways information about customers comes into a business, where and how this data is stored and how it is used. Banks, for instance, may interact with customers in a myriad of different ways including mail campaigns, web-sites, brick-and-mortar branches, call centers, mobile sales force staff and marketing and advertising efforts. In reality all these systems link up each of these points.

14.2. Data Warehouse and Data Mining

As mentioned earlier, the banks are sitting on a wealth of data. Data warehouse, the technology system, is the core of any decision support system and hence of the CRM.

The Analytical Datamart is derived from the Data Warehouse through the following raw data processing: data selection, data extraction, and data verification and rectification.

14.3. Marketing Campaigns

After analysing strategic and analytical CRM, the concentration should be equally important on operational aspects.

Bank marketing in general and Customer Relationship Management (CRM) in particular are of vital importance for Indian banks particularly in the current context when banks are facing tough competition from other agencies, both local and foreign, that offer value added services. Competition is confined not only to resource mobilization but also to lending and other revenue generating areas of services offered by banks. Under the circumstances, it has become essential to develop a close relationship with valued customers and come out with innovative measures to satisfy their needs. Customer expectations for quality services and returns are increasing rapidly and, therefore, quality in future will be the sole determinant of successful banking corporations. It is thus high time that Indian banks organically realize the imperative of proactive Bank Marketing and Customer Relationship Management and take systematic steps in this direction.

14.4. Marketing Approach

Banking industry is essentially a service industry which provides various types of banking and allied services to its clients. Bank customers are such persons and organizations that have surplus or shortage of funds and those who need various types of financial and related services provided by the banking sector. These customers belong to different strata of economy, different geographical locations and different professions and businesses.

Naturally, the need of each individual group of customers is distinct from the needs of other groups. It is, therefore, necessary to identify different homogenous groups and even sub-groups of customers, and then with utmost precision determine their needs, design schemes to suit their exact needs, and deliver them most efficiently.

Banks generally have been working out various services and products at the level of the Head Office and these are traded through their retail outlets (branches) to different customers at the grassroots level. This is the so called "top down" approach. However, bank marketing requires a change in this traditional outlook. It should be "bottom to top" approach with customers at the grassroots level as the focal point for working out various products/ schemes to suit the needs of different homogenous groups of customers. Thus, bank marketing approach, in general, is a group or 'collective' approach.

Customers Relationship Management, on the other hand, is an individualistic approach which concentrates on certain select customers from the homogeneous groups, and develops sustainable relationship with them for adding value to the bank. This may be termed as a 'selective' approach.

Thus, bank marketing concept, whether 'collective' approach or "selective" approach, is a fundamental recognition of the fact that banks need customer oriented approach. In other words, bank marketing is the design and delivery of customer needed services worked out by keeping in view the corporate objectives of the bank and environmental constraints.

Banking Industry is one of the most important service industries which touch the lives of millions of people. Its service is unique both in social and economic points of view of a nation. Earlier the attitude of banking service was that it was not professional to sell one's services and was unnecessary in the sense that traditional relationships and quality of products were sufficient to carry forward the tasks.

14.5. Chapter Summary

Banks have started to focus on Marketing their products through Customers Relationship Management, Call centres, Analytics of data, marketing campaigns, and all other possible ways. Technology supports these initiatives in all possible ways and much more technological innovations are in the pipeline to help the banks marketing their products.

*****

Chapter 15. Anti-Money Laundering

Generally the term Money-laundering is confused with converting black money into white. Conversion of black money into white is definitely an illegal activity, but not under the Anti Money Laundering laws, but under different laws say Income Tax Act.

Another related term confused with Money Laundering is Hawala. This is also an illegal activity. Any foreign currency is to be converted into domestic currency only through approved banking channels. If otherwise converted it is Hawala. For instance if ABC borrows US$ 1,000 from his friend XYZ and pays his Indian Rupee equivalent, it is hawala. This is also illegal under FERA or FEMA or equivalent laws in other countries. Again this is not money laundering.

Money laundering is the process of concealing the source of money obtained by illicit means. The methods by which money may be laundered are varied and can range in sophistication. Many regulatory and governmental authorities quote estimates each year for the amount of money laundered, either worldwide or within their national economy. In 1996, the International Monetary Fund estimated that two to five percent of the worldwide global economy involved laundered money. However, the Financial Action Task Force on Money Laundering (FATF), an intergovernmental body set up to combat money laundering, stated that "overall it is absolutely impossible to produce a reliable estimate of the amount of money laundered and therefore the FATF does not publish any figures in this regard". Academic commentators have likewise been unable to estimate the volume of money with any degree of assurance.

Regardless of the difficulty in measurement, the amount of money laundered each year is in the billions (US dollars) and poses a significant policy concern for governments. As a result, governments and international bodies have undertaken efforts to deter, prevent and apprehend money launderers. Financial institutions have likewise undertaken efforts to prevent and detect transactions involving dirty money, both as a result of government requirements and to avoid the reputational risk involved.

15.1. Methods

Money laundering often occurs in three steps: first, cash is introduced into the financial system by some means ('placement'); the second involves carrying out complex financial transactions in order to camouflage the illegal source ('layering'); and, the final step entails acquiring wealth generated from the transactions of the illicit funds ('integration'). Some of these steps may be omitted, depending on the circumstances; for example, non-cash proceeds that are already in the financial system would have no need for placement.

Money laundering takes several different forms, although most methods can be categorized into one of a few types. These include "bank methods, smurfing [also known as structuring], currency exchanges, and double-invoicing".

- **Structuring**: Often known as 'smurfing', is a method of placement by which cash is broken into smaller deposits of money, used to defeat suspicion of money laundering and to avoid anti-money laundering reporting requirements. A sub-component of this is to use smaller amounts of cash to purchase bearer instruments, such as money orders, and then ultimately deposit those, again in small amounts.
- **Bulk cash smuggling**: Physically smuggling cash to another jurisdiction, where it will be deposited in a financial institution, such as an offshore bank, with greater bank secrecy or less rigorous money laundering enforcement.
- **Cash-intensive businesses**: A business typically involved in receiving cash will use its accounts to deposit both legitimate and criminally derived cash, claiming all of it as legitimate earnings. Best suited is a service business. As such business has no variable costs, it is hard to detect revenues-costs discrepancies. Examples are parking buildings, strip clubs, tanning beds or a casino.
- **Trade-based laundering**: Under- or over-valuing invoices in order to disguise the movement of money.
- **Shell companies and trusts**: Trusts and shell companies disguise the true owner of money. Trusts and corporate vehicles, depending on the jurisdiction, need not disclose their true, beneficial, owner.
- **Round-tripping**: Money is deposited in a controlled foreign corporation offshore, preferably in a tax haven where minimal records are kept, and then shipped back as a Foreign Direct Investment, exempt from taxation.

- **Bank capture**: Money launderers or criminals buy a controlling interest in a bank, preferably in a jurisdiction with weak money laundering controls, and then move money through the bank without scrutiny.
- **Casinos**: An individual will walk into a casino with cash and buy chips, play for a while and then cash in his or her chips, for which he or she will be issued a check. The money launderer will then be able to deposit the check into his or her bank account, and claim it as gambling winnings.
- **Real estate**: Real estate may be purchased with illegal proceeds, then sold. The proceeds from the sale appear to outsiders to be legitimate income. Alternatively, the price of the property is manipulated; the seller will agree to a contract that under-represents the value of the property, and will receive criminal proceeds to make up the difference.
- **Black salaries**: Companies might have unregistered employees without a written contract who are given cash salaries. Black cash might be used to pay them.
- **Fictional loans**

15.2. Enforcement

Anti-money laundering (AML) is a term mainly used in the financial and legal industries to describe the legal controls that require financial institutions and other regulated entities to prevent, detect and report money laundering activities. Anti-money laundering guidelines came into prominence globally as a result of the formation of the Financial Action Task Force (FATF) and the promulgation of an international framework of anti-money laundering standards. These standards began to have more relevance in 2000 and 2001 after FATF began a process to publicly identify countries that were deficient in their anti-money laundering laws and international cooperation, a process colloquially known as "name and shame".

An effective AML program requires a jurisdiction to have criminalized money laundering, given the relevant regulators and police the powers and tools to investigate; be able to share information with other countries as appropriate; and require financial institutions to identify their customers, establish risk-based controls, keep records, and report suspicious activities.

15.3. Criminalizing money laundering:

The elements of the crime of money laundering are set forth in the United Nations Convention Against Illicit Traffic in Narcotic Drugs and Psychotropic Substances and Convention against Transnational Organized Crime. It is knowingly engaging in a financial transaction with the proceeds of a crime for the purpose of concealing or disguising the illicit origin of the property.

15.4. The role of financial institutions:

Today, most financial institutions globally, and many non-financial institutions, are required to identify and report transactions of a suspicious nature to the financial intelligence unit in the respective country. For example, a bank must verify a customer's identity and, if necessary, monitor transactions for suspicious activity. This is often termed as KYC – "know your customer". This means, to begin with, knowing the identity of the customers, and further, understanding the kinds of transactions in which the customer is likely to engage. By knowing one's customers, financial institutions will often be able to identify unusual or suspicious behavior, termed anomalies, which may be an indication of money laundering.

Bank employees, such as tellers and customer account representatives, are trained in anti-money laundering and are instructed to report activities that they deem suspicious. Additionally, anti-money laundering software filters customer data, classifies it according to level of suspicion, and inspects it for anomalies. Such anomalies would include any sudden and substantial increase in funds, a large withdrawal, or moving money to a bank secrecy jurisdiction. Smaller transactions that meet certain criteria may also be flagged as suspicious. For example, structuring can lead to flagged transactions. The software will also flag names that have been placed on government "blacklists" and transactions involving countries that are thought to be hostile to the host nation. Once the software has mined data and flagged suspect transactions, it alerts bank management, who must then determine whether to file a report with the government.

15.5. Value of enforcement costs and associated concerns

The financial services industry has become more vocal about the rising costs of antimoney laundering regulation, and the limited benefits that they claim it appears to bring. The Economist magazine has become increasingly vocal in its criticism of such regulation, particularly with reference to countering terrorist financing, referring to it as a "costly failure", although concedes that the rules to combat money laundering are more effective.

However, there is no precise measurement of the costs of regulation balanced against the harms associated with money laundering and given the evaluation problems involved in assessing such an issue, it is unlikely the effectiveness of terror finance and money laundering laws could be determined with any degree of accuracy. Government-linked economists have noted the significant negative effects of money laundering on economic development, including undermining domestic capital formation, depressing growth, and diverting capital away from development.

Data privacy has also been raised as a concern. A European Union working party, for example, has announced a list of 44 recommendations to better harmonize, and if necessary pare back, the money laundering laws of EU member states to comply with fundamental privacy rights. In the United States, groups such as the American Civil Liberties Union have expressed concern that money laundering rules require banks to report on their own customers, essentially conscripting private businesses "into agents of the surveillance state".

In any event, many countries are obligated by various international instruments and standards, such as the United Nations Convention Against Illicit Traffic in Narcotic Drugs and Psychotropic Substances, the Convention against Transnational Organized Crime, and the United Nations Convention against Corruption, and the recommendations of the FATF to enact and enforce money laundering laws in an effort to stop narcotics trafficking, international organised crime, and corruption. Other countries, such as Mexico, which are faced with significant crime problems believe that anti-money laundering controls could help curb the underlying crime issue.

15.6. Organizations working against money laundering:

Formed in 1989 by the G7 countries, the FATF is an intergovernmental body whose purpose is to develop and promote an international response to combat money laundering. The FATF Secretariat is housed at the headquarters of the OECD in Paris. In October 2001, FATF expanded its mission to include combating the financing of terrorism. FATF is a policy-making body, which brings together legal, financial and law enforcement experts to achieve national legislation and regulatory AML and CFT reforms. Currently, its membership consists of 34 countries and territories and two regional organizations. In addition, FATF works in collaboration with a number of international bodies and organizations. These entities have observer status with FATF, which does not entitle them to vote, but permits full participation in plenary sessions and working groups.

FATF has developed 40 Recommendations on money laundering and 9 Special Recommendations regarding terrorist financing. FATF assesses each member country against these recommendations in published reports. Countries seen as not being sufficiently compliant with such recommendations are subjected to financial sanctions.

FATF's three primary functions with regard to money laundering are:

1. Monitoring members' progress in implementing anti-money laundering measures.
2. Reviewing and reporting on laundering trends, techniques and countermeasures.
3. Promoting the adoption and implementation of FATF anti-money laundering standards globally.

The FATF currently comprises 34 member jurisdictions and 2 regional organisations, representing most major financial centres in all parts of the globe.

The United Nations Office on Drugs and Crime maintains the International Money Laundering Information Network, a website that provides information and software for anti-money laundering data collection and analysis. The World Bank has a website in which it provides policy advice and best practices to governments and the private sector on anti-money laundering issues.

15.7. Laws and enforcement by region

Many jurisdictions adopt a list of specific predicate crimes for money laundering prosecutions, while others criminalize the proceeds of any serious crime.

Afghanistan

The Financial Transactions and Reports Analysis Center of Afghanistan (FinTRACA) was established as a Financial Intelligence Unit (FIU) under the Anti Money Laundering and Proceeds of Crime Law passed by decree late in 2004. The main purpose of this law is to protect the integrity of the Afghan financial system and to gain compliance with international treaties and conventions. The Financial Intelligence Unit is a semi-independent body that is administratively housed within the Central Bank of Afghanistan (Da Afghanistan Bank). The main objective of FinTRACA is to deny the use of the Afghan financial system to those who obtained funds as the result of illegal activity, and to those who would use it to support terrorist activities.

To meet its objectives, the FinTRACA collects and analyzes information from a variety of sources. These sources include entities with legal obligations to submit reports to the FinTRACA when a suspicious activity is detected, as well as reports of cash transactions above a threshold amount specified by regulation. Also, FinTRACA has access to all related Afghan government information and databases. When the analysis of this information supports the supposition of illegal use of the financial system, the FinTRACA works closely with law enforcement to investigate and prosecute the illegal activity. FinTRACA also cooperates internationally in support of its own analyses and investigations and to support the analyses and investigations of foreign counterparts, to the extent allowed by law. Other functions include training of those entities with legal obligations to report information, development of laws and regulations to support national-level AML objectives, and international and regional cooperation in the development of AML typologies and countermeasures.

Australia

AUSTRAC (Australian Transaction Reports and Analysis Centre) is Australia's anti-money laundering and counter-terrorism financing regulator and specialist financial intelligence unit.

The Anti-Money Laundering & Counter Terrorism Financing 2006 (AMLCTF) is the principal legislative instrument, although there are also offence provisions introduced into the Crimes Act 1901 (Cth). Upon its introduction the AMLCTF was to be further amended by a second tranche of reforms to extend inter alia to other commercial contexts such as real estate agents, but those further reforms have since not been effectuated. AUSTRAC works collaboratively with Australian industries and businesses in their compliance with anti-money laundering and counter-terrorism financing legislation. Financial institutions in Australia are required to track significant cash transactions (greater than A$10,000.00 or equivalent in physical cash value) that can be used to finance terrorist activities in and outside Australia's borders and report them to AUSTRAC.

Bangladesh

In Bangladesh, this issue has been dealt with by the Prevention of Money Laundering Act, 2002 (Act No. VII of 2002). In terms of section 2, "Money Laundering means:

A. Properties acquired or earned directly or indirectly through illegal means;
B. Illegal transfer, conversion, concealment of location or assistance in the above act of the properties acquired or earned directly of indirectly through legal or illegal means".

In this Act, 'properties' means movable or immovable properties of any nature and description.
To prevent these Illegal uses of money, the Bangladesh government has introduced the Money Laundering Prevention Act. The Act was last amended in the year 2009 and all the financial institutes are following this act. Till today there are 26 circulars issued by Bangladesh Bank under this act. To prevent money laundering, a banker must do the following:

- While opening a new account, the account opening form should be duly filled up by all the information of the customer.
- The KYC has to be properly filled.
- The Transaction Profile (TP) is mandatory for a client to understand his/her transactions. If needed, the TP has to be updated at the client's consent.
- All other necessary papers should be properly collected along with the voter ID card.
- If any suspicious transaction is noticed, the Branch Anti Money Laundering Compliance Officer (BAMLCO) has to be notified and accordingly the Suspicious Transaction Report (STR) has to be done.
- The cash department should be aware of the transactions. It has to be noted if suddenly a big amount of money is deposited in any account.

Proper documents will be required if any client does this type of transaction.

- Structuring, over/ under invoicing is another way to do money laundering. The foreign exchange department should look into this matter cautiously.
- If in any account there is a transaction exceeding 7.00 lakh in a single day that has to be reported as Cash Transaction Report (CTR).
- All bank officials must go through all the 26 circulars and use them.

Canada

FINTRAC (Financial Transaction and Reports Analysis Centre of Canada) is responsible for investigation of money and terrorist financing cases that are originating from or destined for Canada. The financial intelligence unit was created by the amendment of the Proceeds of Crime (Money Laundering) Act in December 2001 and created the Proceeds of Crime (Money Laundering) and Terrorist Financing Act.

Financial institutions in Canada are required to track large cash transactions (daily total greater than CAD$10,000.00 or equivalent value in other currencies) that can be used to finance terrorist activities in and beyond Canada's borders and report them to FINTRAC.

European Union

The EU directive 2005/60/EC "on the prevention of the use of the financial system for the purpose of money laundering and terrorist financing" tries to prevent such crime by requiring banks, real estate agents and many more companies to investigate and report usage of cash in excess of €15,000. The earlier EU directives 91/308/EEC and 2001/97/EC also relate to money laundering.

India

The Prevention of Money-Laundering Act, 2002 came into effect on 01st July 2005.

Section 12 (1) prescribes the obligations on banks, financial institutions and intermediaries (a) to maintain records detailing the nature and value of transactions which may be prescribed, whether such transactions comprise of a single transaction or a series of transactions integrally connected to each other, and where such series of transactions take place within a month; (b) to furnish information of transactions referred to in clause (a) to the Director within such time as may be prescribed and t records of the identity of all its clients. Section 12 (2) prescribes that the records referred to in sub-section (1) as mentioned above, must be maintained for ten years after the transactions finished. It is handled by the Indian Income Tax Department.

The provisions of the Act are frequently reviewed and various amendments have been passed from time to time.

The recent activity in money laundering in India is through political parties, corporate companies and the shares market. It is investigated by the Indian Income Tax Department.

Bank accountants must record all the transactions whose amount will be more than ₹. 10 Lakhs. Bank accountants must maintain this records for 10 years. Banks will also make cash transaction reports (CTRs) and Suspicious transaction reports whose amounts are more than ₹. 10 Lakhs within 7 days of doubt. This report will be submitted to enforcement directorate and income tax department.

United Kingdom

Money laundering and terrorist funding legislation in the UK is governed by four Acts of primary legislation:-

- Terrorism Act 2000
- Anti-terrorism, Crime and Security Act 2001
- Proceeds of Crime Act 2002
- Serious Organised Crime and Police Act 2005
- Money Laundering Regulations 2007

Money Laundering Regulations are designed to protect the UK financial system. If a business is covered by these regulations then controls are put in place to prevent it being used for money laundering.

The Proceeds of Crime Act 2002 contains the primary UK anti-money laundering legislation, including provisions requiring businesses within the 'regulated sector' (banking, investment, money transmission, certain professions, etc.) to report to the authorities suspicions of money laundering by customers or others.

Money laundering is widely defined in the UK. In effect any handling or involvement with any proceeds of any crime (or monies or assets representing the proceeds of crime) can be a money laundering offence. An offender's possession of the proceeds of his own crime falls within the UK definition of money laundering. The definition also covers activities which would fall within the traditional definition of money laundering as a process by which proceeds of crime are concealed or disguised so that they may be made to appear to be of legitimate origin.

Unlike certain other jurisdictions (notably the USA and much of Europe), UK money laundering offences are not limited to the proceeds of serious crimes, nor are there any monetary limits, nor is there any necessity for there to be a money laundering design or purpose to an action for it to amount to a money laundering offence. A money laundering offence under UK legislation need not involve money, since the money laundering legislation covers assets of any description. In consequence any person who commits an acquisitive crime (i.e. one from which he obtains some benefit in the form of money or an asset of any description) in the UK will inevitably also commit a money laundering offence under UK legislation.

This applies also to a person who, by criminal conduct, evades a liability (such as a taxation liability) – referred to by lawyers as "obtaining a pecuniary advantage" – as he is deemed thereby to obtain a sum of money equal in value to the liability evaded.
The principal money laundering offences carry a maximum penalty of 14 years imprisonment.

Secondary regulation is provided by the Money Laundering Regulations 2003, which was replaced by the Money Laundering Regulations 2007. They are directly based on the EU directives 91/308/EEC, 2001/97/EC and 2005/60/EC.

One consequence of the Act is that solicitors, accountants, tax advisers and insolvency practitioners who suspect (as a consequence of information received in the course of their work) that their clients (or others) have engaged in tax evasion or other criminal conduct from which a benefit has been obtained, are now required to report their suspicions to the authorities (since these entail suspicions of money laundering). In most circumstances it would be an offence, 'tipping-off', for the reporter to inform the subject of his report that a report has been made. These provisions do not however require disclosure to the authorities of information received by certain professionals in privileged circumstances or where the information is subject to legal professional privilege. Others that are subject to these regulations include financial institutions, credit institutions, estate agents (which includes chartered surveyors), trust and company service providers, high value dealers (who accept cash equivalent to €15,000 or more for goods sold), and casinos.

Professional guidance (which is submitted to and approved by the UK Treasury) is provided by industry groups including the Joint Money Laundering Steering Group, the Law Society. and the Consultative Committee of Accountancy Bodies (CCAB). However there is no obligation on banking institutions to routinely report monetary deposits or transfers above a specified value. Instead reports have to be made of all suspicious deposits or transfers, irrespective of their value.

The reporting obligations include reporting suspicions relating to gains from conduct carried out in other countries which would be criminal if it took place in the UK. Exceptions were later added to exempt certain activities which were legal in the location where they took place, such as bullfighting in Spain.

There are more than 200,000 reports of suspected money laundering submitted annually to the authorities in the UK (there were 240,582 reports in the year ended 30 September 2010 – an increase from the 228,834 reports submitted in the previous year). Most of these reports are submitted by banks and similar financial institutions (there were 186,897 reports from the banking sector in the year ended 30th September 2010).

Although 5,108 different organisations submitted suspicious activity reports to the authorities in the year ended 30 September 2010 just four organisations submitted approximately half of all reports, and the top 20 reporting organisations accounted for three-quarters of all reports.

The offence of failing to report a suspicion of money laundering by another person carries a maximum penalty of 5 years imprisonment.

Bureaux de change

All UK Bureaux de change are registered with Her Majesty's Revenue and Customs which issues a trading licence for each location. Bureaux de change and money transmitters, such as Western Union outlets, in the UK fall within the 'regulated sector' and are required to comply with the Money Laundering Regulations 2007. Checks can be carried out by HMRC on all Money Service Businesses.

United States

The US is the pioneer in AML regulations and most of the other countries follow suit. The approach in the United States to stopping money laundering is usefully broken into two areas: preventive (regulatory) measures and criminal measures.

Preventive

In an attempt to prevent dirty money from entering the US financial system in the first place, the United States Congress passed a series of laws, starting in 1970, collectively known as the Bank Secrecy Act. These laws, contained in sections 5311 through 5332 of Title 31 of the United States Code, require financial institutions, which under the current definition include a broad array of entities, including banks, credit card companies, life insurers, money service businesses and broker-dealers in securities, to report certain transactions to the United States Treasury. Cash transactions in excess of US$10,000 must be reported on a currency transaction report (CTR), identifying the individual making the transaction as well as the source of the cash. The US is one of the few countries in the world to require reporting of all cash transactions over a certain limit, although certain businesses can be exempt from the requirement. Additionally, financial institutions must report transaction on a Suspicious Activity Report (SAR) that they deem 'suspicious', defined as a knowing or suspecting that the funds come from illegal activity or disguise funds from illegal activity, that it is structured to evade BSA requirements or appears to serve no known business or apparent lawful purpose; or that the institution is being used to facilitate criminal activity. Attempts by customers to circumvent the BSA, generally by structuring cash deposits to amounts lower than US$10,000 by breaking them up and depositing them on different days or at different locations also violates the law.

The financial database created by these reports is administered by the U.S.'s Financial Intelligence Unit (FIU), called the Financial Crimes Enforcement Network (FinCEN), which is located in Vienna, Virginia. These reports are made available to US criminal investigators, as well as other FIU's around the globe, and FinCEN will conduct computer assisted analyses of these reports to determine trends and refer investigations.

The BSA requires financial institutions to engage in customer due diligence, which is sometimes known in the parlance as "know your customer". This includes obtaining satisfactory identification to give assurance that the account is in the customer's true name, and having an understanding of the expected nature and source of the money that will flow through the customer's accounts. Other classes of customers, such as those with private banking accounts and those of foreign government officials, are subjected to enhanced due diligence because the law deems that those types of accounts are a higher risk for money laundering. All accounts are subject to ongoing monitoring, in which internal bank software scrutinizes transactions and flags for manual inspection those that fall outside certain parameters. If a manual inspection reveals that the transaction is suspicious, the institution should file a Suspicious Activity Report.

The regulators of the industries involved are responsible to ensure that the financial institutions comply with the BSA. For example, the Federal Reserve and the Office of the Comptroller of the Currency regularly inspect banks, and may impose civil fines or refer matters for criminal prosecution for non-compliance. A number of banks have been fined and prosecuted for failure to comply with the BSA. Most famously, Riggs Bank, in Washington D.C., was prosecuted and functionally driven out of business as a result of its failure to apply proper money laundering controls, particularly as it related to foreign political figures.

In addition to the BSA, the U.S. imposes controls on the movement of currency across its borders, requiring individuals to report the transportation of cash in excess of US$10,000 on a form called Report of International Transportation of Currency or Monetary Instruments (known as a CMIR). Likewise, businesses, such as automobile dealerships, that receive cash in excess of US$10,000 must likewise file a Form 8300 with the Internal Revenue Service, identifying the source of the cash.

On 01st September 2010, the Financial Crimes Enforcement Network issued an advisory on "informal value transfer systems" referencing United States v. Banki.

Criminal sanctions

Money laundering has been criminalized in the United States since the Money Laundering Control Act of 1986. That legislation, contained at section 1956 of Title 18 of the United States Code, prohibits individuals from engaging in a financial transaction with proceeds that were generated from certain specific crimes, known as "specified unlawful activities" (SUAs). Additionally, the law requires that an individual specifically intend in making the transaction to conceal the source, ownership or control of the funds. There is no minimum threshold of money, nor is there the requirement that the transaction succeed in actually disguising the money. Moreover, a "financial transaction" has been broadly defined, and need not involve a financial institution, or even a business. Merely passing money from one person to another, so long as it is done with the intent to disguise the source, ownership, location or control of the money, has been deemed a financial transaction under the law. However, the lone possession of money without either a financial transaction or an intent to conceal is not a crime in the United States.

In addition to money laundering, the law, contained in section 1957 of Title 18 of the United States Code, prohibits spending in excess of US$10,000 derived from an SUA, regardless of whether the individual wishes to disguise it. This carries a lesser penalty than money laundering, and unlike the money laundering statute, requires that the money pass through a financial institution.

According to the records compiled by the United States Sentencing Commission, in 2009, the United States Department of Justice typically convicted a little over 81,000 people; of this, approximately 800 are convicted of money laundering as the primary or most serious charge.

*****

Appendix 1 – Major Islamic Banking Terminologies

Table 6 – Islamic Banking Terms

Term	Meaning
Bai' al 'inah	Sale and buy-back agreement
Bai' bithaman ajil	Deferred payment sale
Bai' muajjal	Credit sale
Bai Salam	A contract in which advance payment is made for goods to be delivered later on.
Dyan	Debt
Gharar	Speculative Transactions
Haraam	Investing in unlawful business
Hibah	Gift
Ijarah	Lease, rent or wage.
Ijarah thumma al bai'	Hire purchase
Ijarah-wal-iqtina	A contract under which an **Islamic bank** provides equipment, building, or other assets to the client against an agreed rental together with a unilateral undertaking by the bank or the client that at the end of the lease period, the ownership in the asset would be transferred to the lessee.
Madharaba	A financial institution provides all the capital and the other partner, the entrepreneur, provides no capital.
Maysir	Ownership depends on predetermined or uncertain event of future
Mudarabah	Profit Sharing – is a contract, with one party providing 100 percent of the capital and the other party providing its specialist knowledge to invest the capital and manage the investment project. Profits generated are shared between the parties according to a pre-agreed ratio. Compared to Musharaka, in a Mudaraba only the lender of the money has to take losses
Murabahah Muajjal	A contract in which the bank earns a profit margin on the purchase price and allows the buyer to pay the price of the commodity at a future date in a lump sum or in installments

Musawamah	*Musawamah* is the negotiation of a selling price between two parties without reference by the seller to either costs or asking price.
Musharakah	Joint Venture - an agreement between two or more partners, whereby each partner provides funds to be used in a venture
Qard hassan/ Qardul hassan	Good loan/ benevolent loan
Riba	Interest
Salaam	Sale
Sharia	Islamic Law
Sukuk	Islamic bonds
Takaful	Islamic insurance
Usury	Collection or payment of interest
Wadiah	Safekeeping
Wakalah	Power of attorney

*****

Appendix 2 – Treasury Terms

Treasury specific terms are given in the table below. Though some of the terms are repeated, for completeness sake they are duplicated.

Accrual Swap	An interest rate swap where interest on one side accrues only when a certain condition is met.
Alternative Trading System (ATS)	Systems that offer additional means of trading compared to established exchanges. They operate electronically (lowering transaction costs) and focus on services that established exchanges do not always provide (e.g. central limit order book, after hours trading or direct access for institutional owners).
AMEX	American Stock Exchange
Arbitrage	Profiting from differences in price when the same security, currency or commodity is traded in two or more markets.
ABA Number	"- a number, usually placed near the upper right corner of checks, which identifies the financial institution on which the check is drawn. The number is used in sorting and clearing checks. The ABA coding system was designed by the American Bankers Association."
Ask	The price at which a security is offered for sale.
Basis point	1/100 of 1 percent, i.e. 0.01% used to express a yield spread or differential; 25 basis points is 0.25 percent. One basis point equals 1/1OOth of one percent, or .0001. For example, 50 basis points are equal to 1/2 percent. Basis points are frequently used to describe spreads or changes in yields of interest rates."
Benchmark	Value used as a reference or means of comparison for measuring the performance of an investment.
Bank Wire	An electronic communications network owned by an association of banks and used to transfer messages between subscribing banks. BankWire also offers a clearing service called CashWire that includes a settlement facility
Basel Agreement	An accord developed during a 1975 meeting in Basel, Switzerland of central bankers of the industrialized nations setting forth guidelines for the supervision of banks. Included are guidelines for minimum capital requirements. The agreement was reached by the Committee on Banking Regulations and Supervisory

	Practices (also known as the Cooke Committee after its chairman, Peter Cooke), meeting under the auspices of The Bank for International Settlements
Beta	A measure of the systematic risks of an asset.
Beneficiary	The person designated to receive funds
Bid/ Offer	A bid indicates a desire to buy a commodity at a given price, whereas an offer indicates a desire to sell a commodity at a given price.
Bond	A bond is a debt instrument and includes the promise of the debtor to repay a sum of money at a certain interest rate over a certain period of time. Most bonds pay a fixed rate of interest for a fixed period of time.
Broker	Intermediary who negotiates deals between banks. In most money centres brokers do not act as intermediaries between banks and commercial users of the market. Brokerage is the commission charged by broker for this service.
Bull/ Bear Market	A bull market is market where prices are rising, opposite to a bear market, where prices are declining.
Call	An option to buy a specific security at a specified price within a designated period.
Call Money and Notice Money	The call money market is an integral part of the Indian Money Market, where the day-to-day surplus funds (mostly of banks) are traded. The money that is lent for one day in this market is known as "Call Money", if it exceeds one day (but less than 15 days) it is referred to as "Notice Money". Banks borrow in this Call market for the following purpose to fill the gaps or temporary mismatches in funds to meet the CRR & SLR mandatory requirements as stipulated by the Central bank to meet sudden demand for funds arising out of large outflows.
CEE	Central and Eastern Europe
Central Counterparty	An intermediary which takes over the obligation of either side in respect of a trade. After clearing with a central counterparty, the two trading parties no longer have an obligation towards each other, but rather towards the central counterparty, which thereby assumes any replacement cost risk resulting from market moves between time of trade and the time of settlement.

Clearing	The process of transmitting, reconciling and in some cases, confirming payment order and the securities transfer prior to settlement. In the context of repos, this can have three separate aspects: confirmation/matching, netting and clearing with the central counterparty.
Collateral	Assets held to secure an obligation.
Compliance	Policing by financial institutions to ensure that applicable regulators rules are obeyed.
Credit risk	The risk of loss from a counterparty that is unwilling or unable to settle its side of a transaction.
Counterparty	The opposite side in a financial transaction (or) the other party in a swap transaction."
Coupon	Interest payment made on a bond.
Cross Rate	An exchange rate for two inactively traded currencies to be determined through relationship to a widely traded third currency.
Customers of Treasury	Financial Institutions, Central Banks, local corporates, multinational corporates, insurance companies.
CUSIP number	A number assigned to securities by the Committee on Uniform Securities Identification Procedures (CUSIP). The identifying numbers and codes are used to record all buy and sell orders
Day Trade	A trade that is entered into and closed out on the same day.
Dealer	A person or business firm acting as a middleman to facilitate distribution of securities or goods. Typically, a dealer buys for his or her own account and sells to a customer from the dealer's inventory. Thus a dealer acts as a principal rather than as an agent. The dealer's profit or loss is the difference between the price he pays and the price he receives for the same security or goods. The same individual or company may, at different times, function as a dealer or as a broker, who buys and sells for his clients' accounts
Delta	The rate of change of the price of a derivative with the price of the underlying asset.
Delta Hedging	A hedging scheme that is designed to make the price of a portfolio of derivatives insensitive to small changes in the price of the underlying asset.

Derivatives	A financial instrument, whose value depends on or is derived from the value of an underlying commodity, security or other derivative instruments.
EONIA	EONIA stands for Euro Overnight Index Average and is an effective overnight rate computed as a weighted average of all overnight unsecured lending transactions in the interbank market, initiated within the euro area by the contributing panel banks.
EURIBOR	EURIBOR stands for Euro Interbank Offered Rate and is the rate at which Euro interbank term deposits within the euro zone are offered by one prime bank to another prime bank.
Eurosystem	The European Central Banks and the national banks of the EU member States which have adopted the EURO.
Exposure	Sensitivity to a source of risk.
Financial Markets	Markets that deal with cashflows over time, where the savings of lenders are allocated to the financing needs of borrowers.
Fed wire	The Federal Reserve System's electronic funds transfer network. Fedwire is used for transferring reserve account balances of depository institutions, and for transferring government securities. Fedwire is also used for the settlement of other clearing systems, such as CHIPS (Clearinghouse Interbank Payments Systems), which engages Fedwire for settlement
Fixing	The settling of the price of a commodity (e.g. gold, foreign exchange rate) at a certain time.
Fixed rate	Calculation of interest as a constant specifies percentage of the principal amount payable over an agreed term.
Floating Rate	Interest rate is periodically determined according to the terms of the transaction (e.g. 3 or 6 month basis).
FTSE 100	Stock index of the 100 largest companies listed at the London Stock Exchange. It is calculated and maintained by FTSE International Ltd.
FTSE International Ltd.	Index provider co-owned by the Financial Times (FT) and the London Stock Exchange (LSE)
Future	Contracts to buy or sell a specific financial instrument at a specific future time at a specified price. Such financial instruments include treasury securities, and certificates of deposit, the prices of which fluctuate with changes in interest rates.

	An agreement to buy or sell a standard quantity of a specific commodity on a future date at an agreed price.
Financial Institutions	A corporation chartered for the purpose of dealing primarily with money, such as deposits, investments, and loans, rather than goods or services
Foreign Exchange Rate	The price of one nation's currency denominated in the currency of another nation. For example, the value of British pounds expressed in U.S. dollars
Gamma	The rate of change of delta with respect to the asset price.
Greeks	Hedge parameters such as delta, gamma, vega, theta and rho.
Hedging	A transaction that reduces the price risk of a commodity position (e.g. Foreign Exchange or Interest Rate position) by making the appropriate offsetting derivative transaction. The purchase or sale of a commodity, security or other financial instrument for the purpose of offsetting the profit or loss of another security or investment. Thus, any loss on the original investment will be hedged, or offset, by a corresponding profit from the hedging instrument
Historical volatility	Volatility estimated on historical data.
IPO	Initial public offering. A company's first offering of stock to the public.
Insider trading	Use of privileged information that, once it becomes public, will move the price of the share by someone to profit from this knowledge, having generally acquired the information through their job. This practice is illegal in most markets.
Intermediary	An institution or person (e.g. a broker) that channels funds from surplus spending organisations to deficit spending organisations.
Interbank Trading	Trading between highly experienced traders in various financial instruments like: Interest Rates, Foreign Exchange, Derivatives etc.
Interest rate risk	This is the exposure due to changes in the levels of interest rates. Changes in the interest rates have an impact on interest bearing on-, and off balance sheet assets and liabilities.

IRS	Stands for Interest Rate Swap and implies the exchange between counterparties of a fixed interest rate and a floating interest rate in a single currency.
ISDA	The International Swaps and Derivatives Association (ISDA) is the global trade association representing leading participants in the privately negotiated derivatives industry, a business which includes interest rate, currency, commodity, credit and equity swaps, as well as related products such as caps, collars, floors and swaptions.
Junk bond	A bond which pays a high yield due to significant credit risk.
Kappa	Please refer vega.
Leverage	Company debt expressed as a percentage of equity capital. High leverage means that debts are high in relation to assets. The equivalent UK term is gearing.
LIBOR	LIBOR stands for the London Interbank Offered Rate and is the rate of interest at which banks borrow funds from other banks, in marketable size, in the London interbank market. The interest rate offered by a specific group of London banks for U.S. dollar deposits of a stated maturity. LIBOR is used as a base index for setting rates of some adjustable rate financial instruments
LIFFE	London International Financial Futures and Options Exchange.
Liquidity risk	The risk of a company's working capital becoming insufficient to meet near term financial demands.
Listing	Acceptance of a share for trading by one of the organised and recognised stock exchanges. Listing increases the liquidity of a share and therefore increases demand from investors. Listing increases the price investors are willing to pay for a share.
Long position	A position which entails ownership or effective ownership of an asset.
Market capitalisation	Value of a corporation as determined by the market price of its issued and outstanding common stock.
Market maker	An institution/dealer who supplies prices and is prepared to buy or sell at those stated bid and ask prices. Market makers are generally large financial institutions.
Market User	Parties which are using various markets to trade commodities or hedging their exposure.

Mark-to-market credit exposure	Credit exposure based upon the current market values of counterparty's obligations.
Mark-to-Market	An accounting procedure by which assets are "marked," or recorded, at their current market value, which may be higher or lower than their purchase price or book value
Money Market	The activity generated by financial institutions that facilitate the purchase, sale, and transfer of lendable funds in the form of short-term debt securities such as promissory notes, collateral loans, and Treasury bills
Mine	Expression sometimes used to indicate that the contracting party is willing to buy at the rate offered by the quoting bank.
Minimum Reserve	All credit institutes and banks must deposit a certain amount of money with their local Central Bank. The amount of this minimum reserve of a credit institute is determined in relation to elements of its balance sheet. The minimum reserve system is intended to pursue the aims of stabilising money market interest rates, creating or enlarging a structural liquidity shortage and possibly contributing to the control of monetary expansion. Compliance with the reserve requirement is determined on the basis of the institutions average daily reserve holdings over a one month maintenance period.
Netting	The reduction of offsetting obligations to a single 'net' obligation.
NYSE	New York Stock Exchange
Option	A financial contract that provides the holder the right but not the obligation to buy or sell a financial asset at a specified price.
Offer	An expression of a willingness to sell something at a given price; opposite of bid
Order book	Centralised markets where prices are determined by an order executi9on algorithm from participants sending firm buy and sell orders.
OTC	Stands for over-the-counter. Bilateral transactions not conducted on a formal exchange. The buying and selling of securities that are not listed on an organized exchange. Trading is handled by dealers through negotiation rather than through the use of a stock exchange's auction system

Panel bank	The contributors to EURIBOR are the banks with the highest volume of business in the euro zone money markets. The panel of banks contributing to EURIBOR consists of: • Banks from EU countries participating in the Euro from the outset • Banks from EU countries not participating in the Euro from the outset • Large international banks from non-EU countries but with important Euro zone operations
Position	A market commitment to go long (buy) or short (sell) a security or commodity. It also refers to the amount of securities or commodities owned (long position) or owed (short position).
Plain Vanilla	A term used to describe a standard deal.
Put	A contract giving the holder the right to sell a specific security at a specified price during a designated period. A put is purchased by someone who thinks the price of the underlying security will go down and who wants to lock in a higher selling price. Opposite of call
Portfolio management	Professional Management of a pool of assets, mainly bonds or/and stocks, for an individual or institutional investor. Performance is measured in comparison with Benchmark Indices.
Primary dealer	Selected credit institution authorised to buy and sell original issuance of government securities in direct dealing with the Treasury.
Primary market	Market for new issues of securities.
Quanto swap	A Quanto Swap is an instrument for taking advantage of the interest differential between two currencies without running an exchange rate risk - similar to a basis swap this transaction has LIBOR/EURIBOR fixings on both legs - but all payments are due in the same currency and there is no payment of the notional amount - the spread on LIBOR remains the same for the total agreed period.
Quotation	The actual price or the bid or ask price of either commodities or futures or options contracts at a particular time.
Reference Credit	The embedded credit risk in credit derivative transactions like credit default swaps or credit linked notes.

Return on equity	Amount, expressed as a percentage, earned on a company's common stock investment for a given period.
Rho	The rate of change of the price of a derivative with the interest rate.
Rate of Exchange	The amount of currency of one nation that may be purchased on a specific date with a specified amount of the currency of another nation."
REPO	It is a transaction in which two parties agree to sell and repurchase the same security. Under such an agreement the seller sells specified securities with an agreement to repurchase the same at a mutually decided future date and a price
Reverse Repo	A repurchase arrangement agreement is a procedure for borrowing money by selling securities to counterparty and agreeing to buy them back later at a slightly higher price. The Repo/ Reverse Repo transaction can only be done at Mumbai between parties approved by Central Bank and in securities as approved by Central Bank (Treasury Bills, Central/ State Government securities). The uses of Repo are: • It helps banks to invest surplus cash • It helps investor achieve money market returns with sovereign risk. • It helps borrower to raise funds at better rates • An SLR surplus and CRR deficit bank can use the Repo deals as a convenient way of adjusting SLR/CRR positions simultaneously. • Central Bank uses Repo and Reverse repo as instruments for liquidity adjustment in the system
Risk	Exposure to uncertainty.
Risk factor	A random variable whose uncertainty represents a source of risk.
Reconciliation	The process of analyzing two related records and, if differences exist between them, finding the cause and bringing the two records into agreement.
S&P 500 (Standard & Poor's)	Stock index of 500 leading American companies.
Settlement	The completion of a payment or the discharge of an obligation between two or more parties. Frequently used

	to refer to the payment or discharge of interbank transactions or a series of prior existing transactions.
Settlement Risk	This risk occurs when a payment is required by counterparty and it is unable or unwilling to effect it. Therefore banks have to establish settlement limits for their counterparties.
Sovereign Risk	The risk in lending directly to a government of a foreign country i.e. that the government will either be unable or unwilling to meet its obligations in the future.
Spot	For immediate delivery.
Spread	The difference between the bid and offer price or rate of a commodity.
Stop-Loss Limit	A market risk limit which curtails losses as they occur.
Swap	An agreement for an exchange of payments between two counterparties at some point(s) in the future and according to a specified formula.
SWIFT	A method of conveying interbank instructions and information world-wide.
TARGET	Trans-European Automated Real-time Gross settlement Express Transfer system. The payment system that will link high value payment systems operated by Central Banks of countries participating in the Euro.
Trade Date	The date a transaction is executed
Theta	The rate of change of the price of an option or other derivative with the passage of time.
Tier one assets	Marketable assets fulfilling certain uniform EURO area-wide eligibility criteria specified by the ECB. Among these criteria are the requirements that they must be denominated in EURO, be issued (or guaranteed) by entities located in EEA countries, and be located in a national central bank of SSS of the EURO area.
Tier two assets	Marketable or non-marketable assets for which specific eligibility criteria are established by the national central banks, subject to ECB approval.
Transfer Risk	The risk in lending directly to a government of a foreign country i.e. whether the government will the freely available foreign currency to repay its debt.
Treasury	Treasury is involved in the trading of certain products like Money Market, Foreign Exchange, Banknotes, Derivatives, etc., in various currencies and has to monitor, control, and make evident of risks involved.

	Furthermore Treasury has to ensure the solvency of the bank at all times.
Treasury Bond	A long-term coupon-bearing instrument issued by the government to finance its debt. Treasury bills, commonly referred to as T-Bills are issued by Government of India against their short term borrowing requirements with maturities ranging between 14 to 364 days. All these are issued at a discount-to-face value. For example a Treasury bill of ` 100.00 face value issued for ` 91.50 gets redeemed at the end of its tenure at ` 100.00. Banks, Primary Dealers, State Governments, Provident Funds, Financial Institutions, Insurance Companies, NBFCs, FIIs (as per prescribed norms), NRIs & OCBs can invest in T-Bills.
Triple A/ Double B (AAA/BB)	Credit Rating by companies like Standard & Poors or Moodys of the creditworthiness of an obligor with respect to a specific financial obligation. Obligors can be rated from AAA (best quality) to D.
Underlier	A primary instrument or variable upon which the value of a derivative instrument depends.
Uptick	An increase in price.
Vega	The rate of change in the price of an option or other derivative with volatility.
Volatility	A measurement of the change in price over a given period.
Wholesale financial market	The financial market which deals with large corporations and institutions.
Yield	A return provided by an instrument.
Yours	Expression sometimes used to indicate that the quoting bank is willing to sell to the contracting bank at quoted rate.
Zero coupon bond	A security issued at discount or one which delivers a single coupon at maturity.

Appendix 3 – Glossary

This author has separately written a book titled "Dictionary of Financial Terms", wherein Myriad of Global Financial Terms are demystified. However some of the important terms are explained below:

Table 7 – Some of the banking terms

Co-obligant(s)	In the case of joint loans the second, third, etc., named borrowers, are called co-obligant(s). All of them combinedly called as Joint Borrowers.
Guarantee	Please refer Surety
Primary Security	The goods for purchase of which the loan is sanctioned is offered as security to the Bank. For instance, in the case of vehicle loan, the vehicle is hypothecated to the bank and it is the primary security. (Please also refer secondary security).
Secondary Security	In addition to the primary security, if additional security is offered to the lender then it is called as secondary security.
Surety	In addition to the borrower, the lenders take surety/ guarantee from an additional person on whom the banks can fall back if the borrower fails to repay.

*****

Appendix 4 – List of Abbreviations

Table 8 – Expansion of the abbreviations used

#	Acronym	Expansion
1.	ABS	Asset Backed Securities
2.	AIRB	Advanced Internal Rating Based
3.	ALM	Asset & Liability Management
4.	AML	Anti-Money Laundering
5.	AMLCTF	Anti-Money Laundering & Counter Terrorism Financing
6.	AUSTRAC	Australian Transaction Reports and Analysis Centre
7.	BAMLCO	Branch Anti Money Laundering Compliance Officer
8.	BG	Bank Guarantee
9.	BS	Balance Sheet
10.	CA	Current Assets
11.	CAMEL	A tool for analysing financial institutions like banks – **C**apital Adequacy, **A**sset Quality, **M**anagement Competence, **E**arnings Ability, **L**iquidity Risk and Sensitivity to Market Risk -
12.	CAR	Capital Adequacy Ratio
13.	CBS	Core Banking System
14.	CL	Current Liabilities
15.	CMA	Credit Monitoring and Analysis
16.	CMO	Collateralised Mortgage Obligation
17.	CRM	Customer Relationship Management
18.	CRR	Cash Reserve Ratio
19.	CTF	Combating Terrorist Financing
20.	CTR	Cash Transaction Report
21.	DA	Demand Acceptance
22.	DFI	Development Financial Institution
23.	DMS	Decision Making System
24.	DP	Drawing Power/ Demand Payment
25.	DSS	Decision Support System
26.	EMI	Equated Monthly Installments
27.	FI	Financial Institution
28.	FII	Foreign Institutional Investors
29.	FinCEN	Financial Crimes Enforcement Network

#	Acronym	Expansion
30.	FINTRAC	Financial Transaction and Reports Analysis Centre of Canada
31.	FinTRACA	Financial Transactions and Reports Analysis Center of Afghanistan
32.	FIU	Financial Intelligence Unit
33.	FSA	Financial Supervision Authority
34.	FTA	Free Trade Agreement
35.	GDP	Gross Domestic Product
36.	HDI	Human Development Index
37.	HY	Half Yearly
38.	IRB	Internal Rating Based
39.	IT	Information Technology
40.	JIT	Just in Time
41.	KCC	Key Cash Credit
42.	KYC	Know Your Customer
43.	LC	Letter of Credit
44.	MBS	Mortgage Backed Securities
45.	MIS	Management Information System
46.	MPBF	Maximum Permissible Bank Finance
47.	MTL	Medium Term Loan
48.	NPA	Non-Performing Asset
49.	NSC	National Savings Certificate
50.	OCC	Open Cash Credit
51.	OD	Overdraft
52.	P&L	Profit and Loss
53.	PC	Packing Credit
54.	PD	Probability of Default
55.	PLS	Profit and Loss Sharing
56.	PO	Purchase Order
57.	PSB	Public Sector Bank
58.	QIB	Qualified Institutional Buyers
59.	QIS	Quarterly Information System
60.	RBI	Reserve Bank of India
61.	SAR	Suspicious Activity Report
62.	SARFAESI	Securitisation and Reconstruction of Financial Assets and Enforcement of Security Interest Act, 2002
63.	SBI	State Bank of India
64.	SIDBI	Small Industries Development Bank of India

#	Acronym	Expansion
65.	SLR	Statutory Liquidity Ratio
66.	SPE	Special Purpose Establishment
67.	SPV	Special Purpose Vehicle
68.	STP	Straight Through Processing
69.	STR	Suspicious Transaction Report
70.	STL	Short Term Loan
71.	SWIFT	Society for Worldwide Interbank Financial Telecommunication
72.	TL	Term Loan
73.	TNW	Tangible Net Worth
74.	UCPDC	Uniform Customs and Practice for Documentary Credits
75.	UK	United Kingdom
76.	US	United States
77.	VaR	Value at Risk
78.	VFM	Value for Money
79.	WC	Working Capital
80.	WTO	World Trade Organisation

*****

Appendix 5 – List of Figures

*****

Appendix 6 – List of Tables

*****

About the Author

http://ramamurthy.jaagruti.co.in/

Dr. Ramamurthy is a versatile personality having experience and expertise in various areas of Banking, related IT solutions, Information Security, IT Audit, Vedas, Samskrit and so on.

His thirst for continuous learning does not subside. Even at the age of late fifties, he did research on an unique topic "Information Technology and Samskrit" and obtained Ph.D. - doctorate degreefrom University of Madras. He is into a project of developing a Samskrit based compiler.

It is his passion to spread his knowledge and experience through conducting classes, training programmes and writing books.

He has already published books:

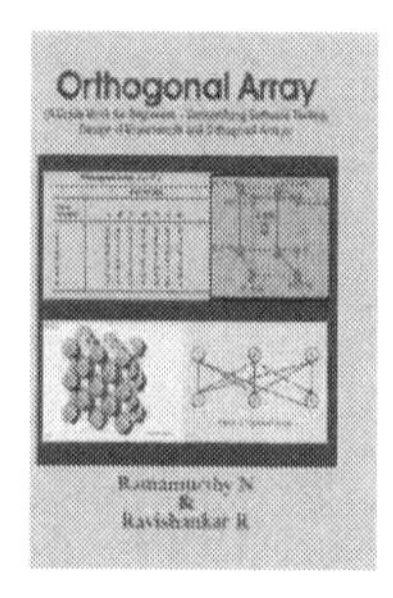

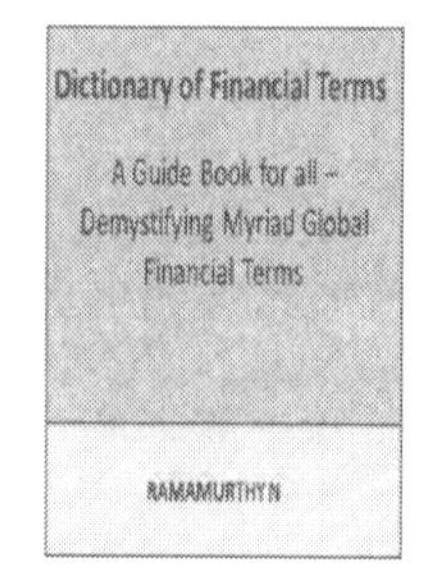

His other books are being published:

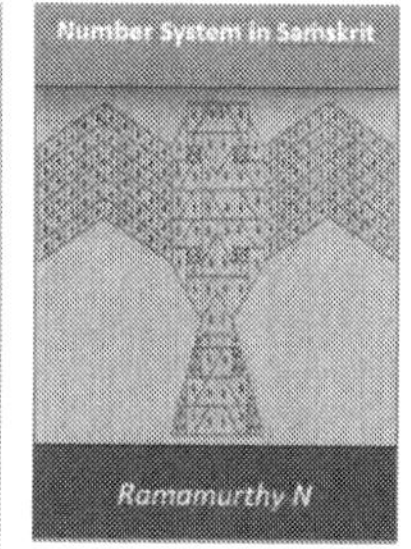

Books being penned - Corporate Finance, Banking – GRC, Information Security in Banks, Sri Devee Mahaatmeeyam, Sri Devi Bhagavatam and many more.

Let us all wish him a long and healthy life so that he could continue his services.

*****

Printed in Great Britain
by Amazon